Heiho Yukan

The Paragon of Military Strategy
volumes 17~20
A Critique of-Merit & Departing for Battle

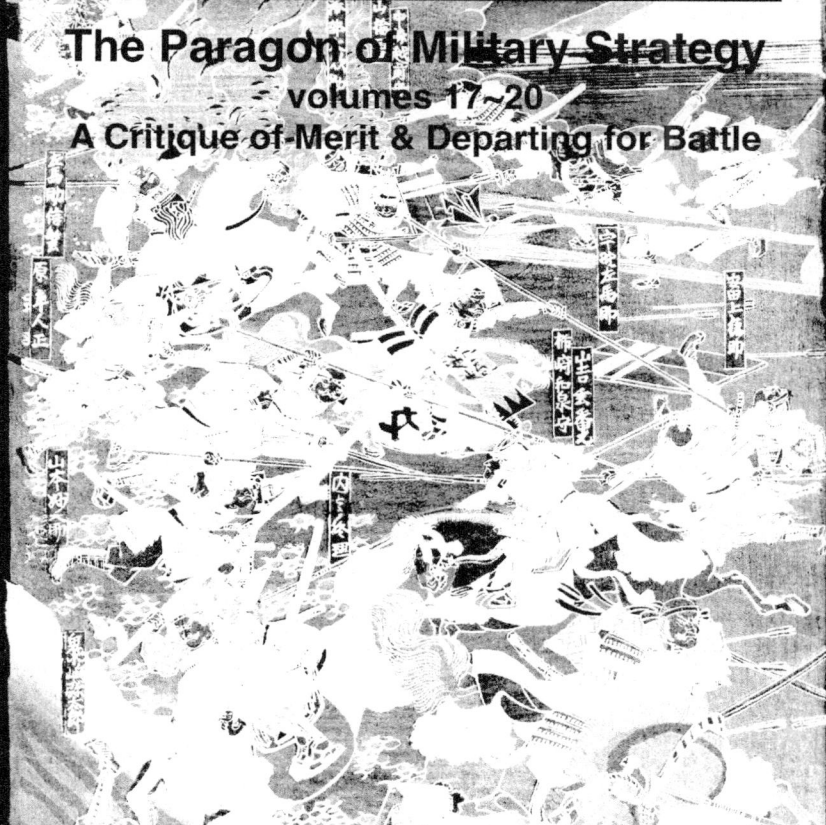

HOJO UJINAGA

Contemporary Japanese: Kazuhiro Iida
English: eric shahan

兵法雄鑑

Heiho Yukan

The Paragon of Military Strategy

Volumes 17-20

手柄批判・出陣

On the Topics of Receiving Merit and Departing for Combat

By Hojo Ujinaga

Transcription, Contemporary Japanese and Illustrations by

Kazuhiro Iida

English by

eric shahan

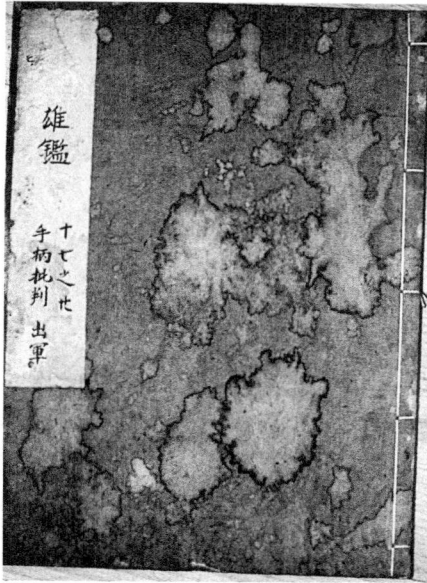

兵法雄鑑…甲州流軍学者、北条氏長により江戸幕府三代将軍、徳川家光に献上された 52 巻に渡る兵法書。

The Paragon of Military Strategy. Written by Hojo Ujinaga of the Koshu School of Military Theory. The fifty-two volumes of this Military Strategy treatise were presented to the third Tokugawa Shogun Tokugawa Iemitsu.

北条氏長…後北条氏の出、小幡景憲に甲州流軍学を学び、継承後に「孫子」などの中国兵法を取り入れ、北条流兵法を創始する。江戸幕府に仕え、最終的に旗本となる。（ウィキペディア、コトバンク等より）

Hojo Ujinaga-Studied the Koshu School of Military Science under Obata Kakgenori and became his successor. Introduced elements of Chinese Military Strategy such as Sun Tzu into it and began the Hojo School of Military Science. A supporter of the Edo Bakufu government he eventually became a retainer. From Wikipedia/Kotobank.

雄鑑

十七ノ二十
十七之廿

手柄批判

出軍 シュツグン

兵法雄鑑 Heiho Yukan

The Paragon of Military Strategy

Volumes 17-20

手柄批判・出陣

On the Topics of Receiving Merit and Departing for Combat

兵法雄鑑抄巻第十七目録

手柄批判上

一 高名之區々

兵法雄鑑妙巻第十七目録

Heiho Yukan Paragon of Military Strategy:

Table of Contents for the Seventeenth Volume

手柄批判上

On the Topic of Receiving Merit First Part

One: Several Considerations on Fame and Renown

1

手柄之批判

一、一番鑓

一、一番鑓トス八大合戦或ハ二百三百ノセ合ニ
弓鉄炮軍終ラスシテ不被射鉄炮ニテ六十間
ナル程近ヨリ八ツカニ三讓リテ退キ支テ
ナリカ（キ時ハ其備ノカサナ形ニ
其時一人進出テ鑓ヲ合スル兵ヲ名付テ
一番鑓ノ高名トスナリ勝頭ハ必時ノ運次
第ナレハ不論此兵ノ忘ハセシ感シテ人ニ

手柄批判

一

一番鑓

一番鑓ト云ハ大合戰或ハ二百三百ノセリ合ニモ

弓鉄炮軍 終テ弓モ不被射、鉄砲モハナサレ

ザル程、近ヨレバタカヒニ護リアイテ退ク事モ

ナリガタキ時ハ其備ノカタチ、ホコヤ形ニナル

其時一人進出テ鑓ヲ合スル兵ヲ名付テ

一番鑓ノ高名ト云ナリ、勝負ハ必時ノ運次

第ナレバ不論此兵ノ心バセヲ感ジテ人ニ

手柄批判

一　　　一番鑓

　　　一番鑓といいますと、(数万同士による)大合戦や二百名から三百名による小規模な合戦においても、弓や鉄砲による遠隔戦闘の後には、弓も鉄砲も次の矢を番えたり、次弾を装填する隙がなく、弓や鉄砲の使用が困難な距離に敵味方の両軍が接近しますので、お互いに目を離す事が出来ず、後備の味方軍とぶつかる為、退却することも困難になった時は、鉾矢形（鋒矢ともいう中国より伝わった八陣の一つ）の陣形を構成します。

　　　その時に一人、真っ先に進み出て鑓で戦う兵士(騎馬武者か徒歩武者かは、ここでは不明。指名された者が務めると他参考文献にある)を一番鑓の高名といいます。勝負は、その時の運にもよりますので、あれこれ議論するまでもなく、この兵士の心意気を汲み取り、誰よりも勇気があると褒め称えるものであります。

Critique of Honor and Merit

One: Ichiban Yari/ First Spear

The term Ichiban Yari refers to a designation given to a Samurai in a large scale battle with tens of thousands of soldiers as well as one involving a small scale battle with just a few hundred warriors. Following the long distance fighting with Yumi (bow) and Teppo (musket) both sides will have advanced toward each other sufficiently so that nocking the next arrow or reloading the next musket ball is impossible. Now that the two sides are at a distance that the Yumi and Teppo cannot be used, neither side can risk looking away from the other. This could also apply to situation where your forces are unable to withdraw as you would run into troops on your own side that are behind you.

Whatever the situation may be you should form your regiment into Hokoyagata, one of the eight formations originating in China resembling and the end of a spear. Amongst the soldiers in the formation the one positioned at the very front, in all likelihood a mounted Samurai with a long spear (This is not entirely clear, this Samurai could well be on foot. Whatever the case may be he is appointed by the commander according to other sources.) is referred to as Ichiban Yari no Komyo, or Renowned First Spear. The fact that victory or defeat in the ensuing battle all depends on how this man performs is not really a matter of debate as all the other troops in the unit will drink in his fighting spirit. This person is thus extoled as a heroic warrior.

スハリヌタル處ヲおムルセ縦ハ勝軍人ソワタ

ストモ此人ヲ英雄之武士ト云ヘシ

二番鑓

二番鑓ト云ハ右ノ一番鑓ニツ丶イテ鑓ノ

一番鑓

入ルヲ二番鑓ト云也是又ニツトラヌ高ク右ナリ

サテ三番鑓ト云亨ハ大形是ナシ子細ハ二ノ

鑓合ヲハレハヤ何カメニツクツレ色付テ惣アリ

ナレ々リ鑓脇付リ鑓下クツレキハ鑓脇トスハ

一テ鑓合入ル人ニサレツ丶イ―テ刀或ハ鉄炮ニテ

スグレタル 處（トコロ）ヲホムル（褒ムル）也、縦（タトエ）バ勝軍（カチイクサニ）人ヲウタ

ズトモ此人ヲ英雄之武士ト云ベシ

二番鑓

二番鑓ト云ハ右ノ一番鑓ニツゝイテ鑓（続ィテ）

ヲ入ルヲ二番鑓ト云也、是又ヲトラヌ（コレ劣ラヌ）高名ナリ、

サテ三番鑓ト云事ハ大形（オオカタ）是（コレ）無シ、子細ハ一二ノ

鑓合ヲワレ（終ワレ）バ、ハヤ何ガタニゾ（方）クツレ（崩レ）色付テ惣カゝリ（総ガカリ）

ナレバナリ、鑓脇付リ（ヤリワキニツケ）、鑓下、クツシキハ（崩シ際）、鑓脇ト云ハ

一二ノ鑓合スル人ニサシツゝイテ（サシ続イテ）刀或ハ鉄砲ニテ

仮に、一番鑓の高名を得た者が敵を討ち取らなくとも、一番鑓となった人を英雄の武士と讃えるべきです。

二番鑓

二番鑓とは、一番鑓に続いて鑓で突撃する者を二番鑓といいます。これもまた一番鑓に劣らない功名です。

さて、三番鑓というものは全く存在しません。何故かと申しますと、一番鑓と二番鑓の戦いが（勝利で）終われば、もはや敵陣は陣形を乱して敗色濃厚となり、此方は総攻撃に出るからです。

二番鑓以降の者は、鑓脇に付きます。鑓下、崩し際（鑓下の功名、崩し際の功名）

鑓脇といいますのは、一番鑓、二番鑓の鑓で戦う者に続いて、刀や鉄砲などで敵を攻撃する者で、刀鑓脇又は、弓鉄砲鑓脇といいます。

In any event, even if the person designated as Renowned First Spear does not take down any of the enemy personally, the Samurai assigned this honor should receive praise as a valiant Bushi.

Niban Yari

Second Spear

The position of Second Spear follows the First Spear in attacking the enemy with his spear. This position is in no way inferior to First Spear and is a great honor. As for the position of Third Spear, this designation does not exist. If you were to ask why, the reason is that should the attacks by the First Spear and Second Spear be (successfully) completed then the sense that the enemy regiment is beginning to crumble and is verging on defeat would be apparent. The remaining forces in your unit would then shift to a more general attack.

Those Samurai assigned below Second Spear are known as Yari Waki, or Side Spears. (Among this category are designations such as) Yari Shita, or the achievement of being able to lay an opponent flat out with your spear , as well as Kuzushi Giwa, or the achievement of bringing about a rout.

The title of Side Spear goes to those who fight with spears other than those designated First Spear or Second Spear. Following them those that attack with Katana or Muskets are known as Katana Side Spear in addition to Bow and Musket Side Spear.

ツムルノ刀鑓脇或ハ弓鉄炮鑓脇ト云也

然ニ敵味方トモニ刀ニテ鑓脇ツツムル人鑓

脇ノ一番セ殊更鑓ツ合スル前後ニシヒテ

退キカ又ル敵ツ推シ込鑓下ニテ取ツ鑓下

ノ高名スコシソンキンノツシキハナトニ云ヘシ

此人モシ鑓ノモノノイアホトツヨミノ鑓シモ可

仕故ニ鑓脇ハ上トシ三番鑓ヨリハスコレ（テシ

ナリト云ナリ　次ニ弓鑓脇　次ニ鉄炮鑓脇

ナリ

ツムルヲ刀鑓脇或ハ弓鉄砲鑓脇ト云也

然ニ敵味方トモニ刀ニテ鑓脇ヲツムル人鑓

脇ノ一番也、殊更鑓ヲ合スル前後ニヲヒテ

退キカヌル敵ヲ推シ込、鑓下ニテ打取ヲ鑓下

ノ高名、スコシヲソキヲ、クヅシギハナドト云ベシ

此人モシ鑓ヲモタバ、イカホドツヨミノ鑓ヲモ可

仕、故ニ鑓脇ノ上トシ二番鑓ヨリハ、スコシマシ

ナリト云ナリ次ニ弓鑓脇次ニ鉄砲鑓脇

ナリ

当然ながら、敵味方共に刀で鑓脇をつとめる人が（接近戦に
なり、より戦死の危険を冒しますので）鑓脇の一番となりま
す。

　特に戦闘中に（進退を迷い）退きかねている敵を突進して
討ち取る事を鑓下の高名といい、戦闘に少し遅れ、友軍優勢
で敵勢が崩れはじめたところを攻撃して敵を討ち取る事を崩
し際(の功名)などといいます。このような者を一番や二番の
鑓に就ければ、どれほど頼もしいでしょうか。故に鑓脇の上
として二番鑓より評価が高いものです。その次が弓鑓脇、次
が鉄砲鑓脇の順に手柄となるのです。

It goes without saying that the warriors on your side as well as on the enemy side have Side Spears armed with Katana thus (due to the fact that this is close quarters combat and many will face death in battle) there is the designation of First Side Spear.

In particular, when in the midst of battle against an intractable enemy (and your side is debating between advancing or retreating) a warrior who strikes in viciously and knocks the enemy down flat is honored with the name Renowned Yari Shita. A warrior who is somewhat late joining the fray but who adds crucial strength to the forces on his side and, when the tide of battle is on the cusp of turning in your favor, strikes an enemy combatant down flat is honored with the name Honored Kuzushi Giwa (the Honor of Being the One Who Led the Breaking Point).

Should a person like this serve under the First Spear or Second Spear one can only wonder at how reliable a warrior he would become. For that reason this top position of Side Spear is given higher merit than Second Spear. Following that the order of merit goes next to Bow Side Spear and after that is Musket Side Spear.

場中勝頁高名

場中之勝頁ト云ハ敵味方トモ三二町ヘ々
テ、鉄炮ヲ放シカケ進近テ敵間三十間
ハカリニモナレハハヤ箭軍初テ扱両偸ノ中ヨリ
勇士進出テ弓ヲ射鉄炮ヲハナセハ其間
五六間十ラテハサキ三其中三手頁充人ヘアルヲ
走ヨリ一刀モ切付クルン場中ノ勝頁ト云
其敵ヲウツヲ高ノ名ト云也如斯ナレ刻
ウチタルノ人ハ青ハモノナリトモ同支ナリ

場中勝負髙名
バチュウショウブノコウミョウ

場中之勝負ト云ハ敵味方トモニ二町ヘダ

テヽ鉄炮ヲ放シカケ進近テ敵間三十間

バカリモアレバ、ハヤ箭軍 初テ扨両備ノ中ヨリ
ヤイクサハジマリ　サテ

勇士進出テ弓ヲ射、鉄炮ヲハナセバ其間

五六間ナラデハナキニ其中ニ手負死人アルヲ

走ヨリ一刀モ切付タルヲ場中ノ勝負ト云

其敵ヲウツヲ高名ト云也、如斯ナル刻
カクノゴトク

ウチタルハ青バモノナリトモ同事ナリ
青　歯　者　オナジコト
オナジコト

場中勝負高名

　場中の勝負というのは敵味方共に一～二町(約 100～200m。一町は約 109.09m)隔て、鉄砲隊が撃ち合い、全軍が前進して両軍間の距離が三十間(約 55m。一間は約 1.818 1818m)程になった時に、両軍勢から弓隊が弓矢を射掛け出し、鉄砲隊が更に鉄砲を撃ちながら前進して、更に距離が五～六間(10m前後)になるかならないかに迫った時に敵側の死傷者に矢玉の飛び交う中を駆け寄って一太刀も斬りつけることを場中(矢玉が飛び交う中の意)の勝負といいます。場中(矢玉が飛び交う中)で敵を討ち取る事を高名とするのであります

　(場中の功名)。このようなときに敵を討ち取るのですから、相手が青バ者(お歯黒を付けていない身分の低い者で討ち取っても手柄にならない者。青葉者、青歯者、白歯者と書き、アオバモノと読む。雑兵(ぞうひょう)、小者(こもの)、中間(ちゅうげん)等)であっても手柄になります。

Bachu Shobu no Komyo

Merit for Striking Down an Enemy on an Active Battlefield

(In the space between where armies are closing in on each other)

Striking Down an Enemy as Armies Close on Each Other refers to when your forces and the enemy's forces are one to two Cho apart (A Cho is a unit of distance 109.09 meters). As the two sides fire upon each other with matchlocks and close to a distance of some thirty Ken (A Ken is a unit of measure equivalent to 1.8 meters, so about 55 meters) apart, archers from both sides will begin to launch arrows from their bows as the riflemen continue to fire.

Further, when the distance closes to about five or six Ken (about ten meters) between the armies, despite Samurai being felled by arrows and musket shot, the warriors that run out across to the other side and cut down opposing warriors with one stroke of their Kanata receive Merit for a victory on an active battlefield (amid flying projectiles).

There is merit (known as Honor on an Active Battlefield) granted for taking out an enemy on an Active Battlefield (amidst flying arrows and matchlock balls). In a situation such as this even if the adversary you cut down was an Aobamono, or Blue Teeth/Blue Leaf you will still receive merit.

Note:

Blue Teeth or Blue Leaf is a person of low birth who has not dyed his teeth black, a common practice among people of higher birth. Except in this case the taking of such a low level person's head would result in no merit. Japanese refer to some colors Westerners term green as blue. Blue also has a meaning of pure and unadulterated. The word leaf and teeth are homonyms in Japanese as in English. The Kanji can be written in various ways.

又如此刻場中ニテ味方侍ノ手負テ引

兼ルヲ引ノケテ敵ニ不為討モ同意、

ノ高名ナルヘシ

組討

大物見ナトニ出敵ニ味方モ馬上ニテセリ

合百之ニ馬上ヨリ組テ落其敵ヲツ、ナトル

吉又無煩之高名也

印…

進崩レテヨリ後ニ弃取ヲツハ二七ヒ二ト云ナリ

又如此刻場中ニテ味方 侍 手負テ引
カクノゴトキトキ　　　　　ミカタノサムライテオイ

兼ルヲ引カケテ敵ニ不為討モ同意
　　　　　　　　　ウタセザル

ノ高名ナルベシ

組討

大物見ナドニ出、敵モ味方モ馬上ニテセリ
　　　　　　　　　　　　　　　　　競リ

合有之ニ、馬上ヨリ組テ落、其敵ヲウチトル
コレアル

事、無類之高名也
　　ムルイノコウミョウナリ

印
しるし

追崩シテヨリ後ニ打取タルヲハ、シルシト云ナリ
　　　　　　　　印

19

また、このような場中で負傷して動けない味方を抱きかかえて引き返して敵に討たせないことも同意の功名といえますでしょう。

組討

　大物見（大将自らの威力偵察）などに出たときに敵と遭遇すれば、敵も味方も騎馬で戦うことがあります。この時、馬上で組み合って落ちて敵を組み伏せて討ち取る事は、無類の功名であります。

印（首級）

敵を追崩して討ち取った敵の首を印といいます。

Further, during this time when the armies are entering close range, retrieving a Samurai from your side who has become injured and cannot move would, by the same principles stated above, confer Merit.

Kumi Uchi

Groups on Horseback Fighting Each Other

Should you, quite by chance, come across an O-Monomi, or a Taisho General doing reconnaissance/checking the lay of the land, it is likely that a skirmish will ensue with both friendly and enemy forces mounted on horseback. If you engage with an opponent while mounted and strike him from his horse then hold him down and dispatch him it will result in an almost incalculable amount of Merit.

Shirushi

Shu Kyu

A Rank for a Type of Head Taken

Having broken the enemy's formation and pursued them any enemy heads taken are known as Shirushi.

我等モツレス隨分走廻タルトノシルシノ

首十七八印ト云然ルニ其印ノ中ニ上中

下百必其ウチレタル侍能敵ト見ハ其刀

楊指ロ母衣指物カ何ニテモ取來ルヘシ

其首ノ右ソレランアツメモ殊更母衣武

者ハ其母衣ノトリ來ラサルハ高名ニナラス

ト云也心得ヘシ口傳

撃將

追頭印ノ中ニモ上ノ誉百ト云ド先其敵ノ

我等モヲクレズ随分走　廻タルトノシルシノ

首ナレハ印ト云、然ルニ其印ノ中ニ上中

下有、必其ウタレタル侍能敵ト見バ、其刀

脇指カ母衣指物カ何ニテモ取来ルベシ

其首ノ名ヲシランガタメ也、殊更母衣武

者ハ其母衣ヲトリ来ラザルバ高名ニナラズ

ト云也、心得ベシ口傳

撃將

追頭印ノ中ニモ上ノ誉有ト云ハ先其敵ノ

　我等も気後れせず戦場を随分駆け回って戦い、討ち取った証しとなる首なので印（首級）といいます。当然ながら、その首級の中に上中下のランクがあり、必ず討ち取った侍を手柄になる敵であると見なせば、その侍の刀や脇指、母衣、指物など何でも証拠となる物を首と一緒に持ち帰るべきであります。それは、その首級の名前を調べて手柄になるか審議するためであります。殊更に母衣武者を討った時は、その母衣を取って来なければ、手柄にならないということを心得てください。口伝

As we move about the field of battle from one side to the other without fear or timidity the severed heads serve as evidence of the men we killed. They are known as Shirushi (Rank of importance for heads taken). It goes without saying that within the topic of severed heads there are upper, middle and lower ranks. If you wish to claim that you took the head of a Samurai of a certain rank then you should, without fail, collect evidence to that fact. His Katana, Wakizashi (short sword), Horo (a bamboo frame covered with fabric worn on the back as protection against arrows), finger ornaments and anything else that could serve as evidence should all be carried home along with the head. All these things are essential to determine the name and rank of the Samurai whose head you have taken. You should note that particularly in the case of the head of a warrior wearing a Horo, neglecting to bring the Horo back could result in not being awarded great Merit.

大将軍ヲ討取亥ハ大概追チナレトモ是一

人ノ万人ニモ七ニモナル高名ナレハミヤウカノ武士ト

名付高名ノ第一ナリトハトカリノ沙汰ニ及儀七

次ニ采配ヲ添持求ル頭是又追頭ナリトモ

誉ノ上ト云子細ハ毎弁一取持ノ侍ハ侍大将ノ

足軽大将ノ或ハ組頭物頭ノ物本行ノ印ナルニ

然者何ト敗軍ノ時モ義ノ知リ恩ヲ重ニ

テ命ソカロシモル同心ニ被官付添テ討ニスヤ

モノナリ失更味方ハ追散シテ後ノ勝組ナレハ

大將軍ヲ打取事ハ大概追打ナレドモ是一

人ガ万人ニモマシタル高名ナレバミヤウガノ武士ト
名付、高名ノ第一ナレバ、トカクノ沙汰ニ不及儀也

次ニ采牌ヲ添持来ル頭、是又追頭ナリトモ

譽ノ上トス、子細ハ再拜取持ノ侍ハ、侍大将カ

足輕大将カ或ハ組頭、物頭カ物奉行ノ印ナルベシ

然者何ト敗軍ノ時モ義ヲ知リ恩ヲ重ジ

テ命ヲカロンズル同心被官付　添　テ討ニクキ

モノナリ、殊更味方ハ追散シテ後ノ勝負ナレバ

26

撃将

　追首（逃げる敵を追って殺害して取った首）の中にも上の誉（良い手柄）があるのは、まずその敵の大将を討ち取る時点で大概追い討ちとなっていますが、大将首を取る事自体が、（合戦の勝利となり）万人にも勝る功名となりますので、冥加の武士といい、功名の第一となりますので、兎角その首が追首であることの善悪を評定するに及ばない儀となります。

　次に采牌を所持している者の首もまた、追首で取っても誉れ高い手柄とします。なぜなら、采牌を持つ侍は侍大将か足軽大将、或は組頭物頭か物奉行といった比較的身分の高い者であります。このような（身分の高い）者は、敗軍の時も忠義深く、主恩を重んじて命を軽く投げ出してくれる同心や被官が護衛していて、なかなか討ちにくいものであります。

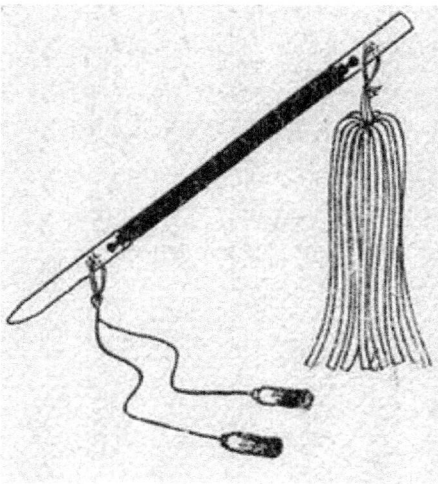

Illustration of a Saihai 采配・采牌 from Wikipedia.

Gekisho

Attacking a General

Within the topic of Oikubi, a head taken after pursuing and cutting down an enemy, the highest possible honor goes to taking the head of a fleeing general. In all likelihood the action of taking the General's head is going to be Oikubi, but as it is a General's head (that will result in victory in that battle) it is enough honor for ten thousand men. A Samurai who takes the head of a Shogun is thereafter referred to as Myoga no Bushi, or divine protector. This is the highest possible honor. In principle the fact that such a head was taken while in pursuit of a fleeing enemy is not taken into consideration when evaluating its validity.

Further, if the head of a Samurai in possession of a Saihai (A lacquered wood stick with paper or leather tassels on the end. See illustration above) is taken during Oikubi this is also classified as a high honor. The reason for this is that a Samurai holding a Saihai is likely the Samurai Taisho, the Ashigaru Taisho or even possibly the group leader/ unit leader/ master-at-arms and therefore possessing a higher status. People of this status are fiercely loyal even when the battle has turned against them. The duty and honor these mid to upper level soldiers feel for their lord is such that they will think nothing of throwing themselves at an opposing force in order to guard their lord. Thus they are rather hard to cut down.

勝メル方ハ馬ヲ引寄キ来テ敵ヲ追語ヽリ

キトヽラント一足ヲ引メニテ乘付間同心被官

頭長大形右ノ通ニテ一人働成ハヽ此所ソヒヽ

サクシテ是ソ上ノホニトス又合戦勝利劍

敵二三十モカヽ〵リ備ヲ見ソナス引取処へ

ケ〵リ圖ソヽトメ敵ソッキ子ラシ我ミウナ

人ニモウメスルハ是又能ホニ〵ナリ剛ノ武士ト

云へヽシ　ハミニ〵キ大〵ニ〵ト〵〵〵

後驅　ヲ〵ヲ〵〵〵〵〵〵〵〵〵

勝タル方ニハ馬ヲ引寄、打乗テ敵ヲ追詰ウ

チトラント一足ヲイダシテ乗付間、同心、被官、
出シ

頭モ大形右ノ通ニテ一人働成ベシ、此所ヲセン
穿

サクシテ是ヲ上ノホマレトス、又合戰勝利刻
鑿　　　　　　　　マタカッセンノショウリノトキ
誉

敵二三十モカタマリ備ヲ見タサズ引取処ヘ
二十〜三十人　　　乱
サズ

カヽリ圍（味方）ヲマトメ敵ヲツキチラシ我モウチ
突キ散シ　　討チ

人ニモウタスルハ是又能ホマレナリ剛ノ武士ト
討タス

云ベシ

後駆

30

殊更、味方は敵軍を追い散して後の戦いですので、勝った方は馬を引寄せて乗り込んで敵を追撃して討ち取ろうと、馬に一跨ぎして乗り込むまでに敵方の同心被官頭も殆どが、右の通り（前述の命を投げ出しての報恩）に一人一人が敵将を此方の追撃から守らんと妨害防戦するものであります。このあたりを評定して采牌持ちの首も上の誉とします。又、合戦勝利のとき、敵が二十〜三十人もかたまって、陣形を乱さずに撤退するところに　味方をまとめて敵を追撃して混乱せしめて自分も敵将兵を討ち、味方にも敵将兵を討たせることは、是又、大変名誉な手柄であります。このような働きをする者は、剛の武士と讃えるべきです。

後駆

Further, with regards to when the forces on your side are in pursuit of the enemy, they will usually approach on horseback and ride into the midst of the fleeing enemy. While charging in with great strides know that the low to mid-level troops will, as was mentioned above, engage in the defensive tactic of throwing themselves at you one by one in an attempt to protect their lord. Taking the head of a Samurai holding a Saihai during such an action would result in the Merit discussed above. Sometimes, during a victorious battle, you find a group of some twenty or thirty odd soldiers attempting to retreat in a formation that has not become ragged. In all likelihood you will attack them as a group with your allies in an effort to throw them into confusion allowing you to take their Shogun's head. If either you, or your compatriots, succeed in taking his head then it will result in a supreme amount of merit being awarded. A person who succeeds in such an action is thereafter known as Go no Bushi, or Steel Warrior.

Okuregake

Being Pursued (Due to not leaving in time)

敵國ヘ深リ働入士卒ノタメニハツクレ口ニ

シテ引トル時殿ヲ為ス元来大剛之侍也殊妙方

午頭テイカヌル武者ノ引ヲケスハ敵ト、フニ

鑓ヲ合スル侍ハ一番鑓ト同意ノ高名ナリ

但シ忠ニセハ鮨句ツヨミハ一番鑓ミ

シタリトス如此刻味方能侍ヲ死ヲテ百之ハ

其首ヲアケ来レカ或其被官ニ下知シテ敵方ヘ

反セマセワニヱ是ツヨキ武士之作法ナリ但

其時ノ様子ニヨルヘキ妄也

敵國ヘ深ク働入、士卒ヲ多クウタセ、ヲクレ<ruby>討<rt>タ</rt></ruby><ruby>セ<rt>セ</rt></ruby><ruby>後<rt>ヲ</rt></ruby>ロニ

シテ引トル時、殿ヲスル事、大剛之侍也、殊味方<ruby>シンガリ<rt></rt></ruby><ruby>ダイゴウノサムライナリ<rt></rt></ruby>

手負テノキカヌ武者ヲ引カケ又ハ敵シトフニ<ruby>退キ兼ヌル<rt></rt></ruby><ruby>死鬭（？）<rt></rt></ruby>

鑓ヲ合スル侍ハ一番鑓ト同意ノ高名ナリ

但シ心バセハ結句ツヨミハ一番鑓ノ覚ヨリハ勝<ruby>ケック剛ミ<rt></rt></ruby>

レタリトス、如此刻味方能侍打死シテ有之バ<ruby>カクノゴトキトキ、ミカタノヨキサムライ、ウチジニ<rt></rt></ruby><ruby>コレアラ<rt></rt></ruby>

其首ヲアゲ来ルカ或、其被官ニ下知シテ敵方ヘ<ruby>アルイハ<rt></rt></ruby>

取セヌヤウニスベシ、是ツヨキ武士之作法ナリ但<ruby>剛キ<rt></rt></ruby>

其時ノ様子ニヨルベキ事也

33

敵國へ深く攻め込んだとき、友軍の士卒が多く討たれて敗色
が濃くなり、やむなく撤退するとき、殿（しんがり）をつとめ
る者は、大剛の侍であります。殊に味方が負傷して動けない
武者を引き受け、又は、追いかけてくる敵と戦う侍の手柄は、
一番鑓と同等となります。但し一番鑓以上の決死の覚悟が必
要なため、心だてを酌まれ、一番鑓より覚えが良いものとな
ります。この状況で殿を務める侍は、味方の侍が討ち死にし
ていれば、その首を取って持ち帰り、敵にとらせないように
するか、或はその侍の被官に命じて敵から守らせようとする
でしょう。是は強い武士のなすべきことであります。但し、
これは、その時の状況によって褒められる場合と褒められな
い場合があります。

This describes a situation whereupon you are deep within enemy controlled territory and many of the Samurai on your side have been cut down. The tides of war are leaning towards defeat for your forces so you have begun to withdraw.

The person who serves as the Shingari, or the rear guard "anchor" is known as the Steel Warrior. In particular, those Samurai that take responsibility for wounded soldiers rendered unable to move and fight off pursuing adversaries receive merit equivalent to that of First Spear. That being said, the person called upon to be Shingari needs to have prepared themselves for death even above and beyond what is required for First Spear. You should fix this fact in your mind. When serving as Shingari under these circumstances, if Samurai on your side are cut down their heads will be sliced off and taken. You have been ordered to prevent that and/or to work with those Samurai in order to serve as a rear guard. That this duty is beyond what is required for first spear should be remembered. Do note that there are occasions where you will receive merit and occasions where you will not.

将付

敵國深リ働合ッレ口ニテ引取去難儀成

剣能主ニッキ候侍是大ナル誉也殊ニ主馬

離ルルニ我下馬ニテ奉乗大成忠切也廿ン

クレ口ノ時着物ナトントニテ有ッ取ッ敵ハ侍モ

剛強成働トスルセ

援出

シレムヤ時敵見崩ニニテ鑓不合トモ味方ノ

中ニテ一騎進出ル侍ハ敵ツガヘハ鑓ッモ可

将付

敵國深ク働入、ヲクレロニシテ引取事難儀成

刻、能主ニツキ候侍、是大ナル誉也、殊ニ主馬

離タルニ我下馬シテ奉乗大成忠功也、付ヲ

クレロノ時着物ナドヲトシテ有ヲ取テ帰ル侍モ

剛強成働トスル也

抜出

オシムカフ時、敵見崩ニシテ鑓不合トモ味方ノ

中ニテ一騎進出ル侍ハ敵ツガヘバ鑓ヲモ　可

将付

　敵國深く攻め込んで、戦況が不利になり、撤退の好機を逸してしまい、引き返す事が困難となったときに良く主将に付き従う侍は、これが大いなる名誉を得ます。殊に主将が馬を離れたときに自分も下馬して主将に付き従うのは多大なる忠義であります。不利な戦況下に主将が着物などを落としているのを取って帰る侍も剛強な活躍をしたとするものです。

抜出

　敵に向かって行くとき、敵が見崩（我が軍を見て、戦う事無く混乱や退却をする事）で戦うことがなくても味方の中から一騎進み出る侍は、敵が弓を番(つが)えば、その時点で敵を討ち取って手柄に出来ますので、是もかなりの名誉となります。

Sho ni Tsuku

Attending to the Shogun

A commander has ventured deep into enemy territory and despite seeing the tide of battle turn unfavorably, misses the chance to withdraw. Any Samurai accompanying the commander at this time can receive a great deal of merit. In particular, should the commander have become separated from his mount you too would dismount and accompany the commander on foot. This would truly show great service and respect to your lord. During the course of these unfortunate circumstances should you retrieve your commander's dropped Kimono, or some such, and succeed and bringing the item home it will be considered an act of conspicuous service for a valiant Samurai.

Nukide

Sudden Withdrawal

In the case where your side launches an attack against the enemy and they, upon seeing the strength of your forces fall into disarray and retreat Samurai from your side may ride out on horseback and attack solo. Should the enemy, in such a case, be nocking an arrow in their bows when the Samurai strikes them merit can be achieved.

仕ナレハ是ニテ能誉ニセ如斯刻ハ崩キワニテ

人ヲ討取ハ場中ノ勝負ニモシントラサル高名

ナントテ敵ヨハ敵ナレハ其所ヲセニサリシテ

鑓下同意ノ高名ト定ルセ

鼻

首ヲ取鼻ヲカリ去ハ場中ノ高名ノ時後詰

ニ衆ニヨリスハタ武者ノアンハ者ナトノ

取処ナキ頭セ又サナクトニ後ノ働ノ心ニカルル

ヲタメナレハ鼻ヲカキ具足ノムナイタメノ間ニ入ル

仕 ナレバ是モ能誉レ也、如斯刻ハ崩ギワニテ
（可（ベキ） ヨキホマレ 斯クノ如キトキ

人ヲ討取ハ場中ノ勝負ニモオトラサル高名
劣（ラザル）

ナレドモ敵ヨハ敵ナレバ其所ヲセンサクシテ
弱 穿 鑿

鑓下同意ノ高名ト定ル也

鼻

首ヲ取、鼻ヲカク事ハ場中ノ高名ノ時、後詰
搔（ク）

ノ衆ニコトハリズバ、ダ武者ノアヲバ者ナドノ
断（リ） 駄 青歯

取処ナキ頭也、又サナクトモ後ノ働ヲ心ニカクル
クビ

タメナレハ鼻ヲカキ、具足ノムナイタノ間ヘ入ル
搔キ 胸板

このような時は、敵の崩れ際に敵を討ち取れば、場中の勝負にも劣らない手柄ですが、敵が弱い敵ですので、そのあたりを審議して鑓下の功名と同等の手柄と定めるものです。

鼻

首を取って鼻を掻き切って持ち帰る事は、場中の功名の時、後方に控えている味方に証人となる了解を取っていなければ、武者の青葉者などの取っても手柄にならない首を取った扱いになります。又、その後の戦いの邪魔にならぬように鼻を切り取って具足の胸板の間にしまう事がある事を必ず知っておいて下さい。

For situations like this where the enemy has broken ranks and you are charging in cutting down opponent's, the merit received is equivalent to that of "victory on a live battlefield." Due to the fact that the opponent is somewhat weak the merit may be established as being equivalent to "downing with a spear."

Hana

Nose

If, during "a victory on a live battlefield," you scrape and cut the nose off of a head you have taken you must have witness from your own side willing to vouch for you. If you do not the head will be treated as if it had come from an Aobamono Musha, or a low ranking Samurai (with teeth not dyed black. Aobamono Musha is Blue Leaf Warrior. In this case blue-leaf refers to a new or young leaf, with blue denoting pure as in white teeth.) Further, you should be very much aware that in order to prevent it getting in the way the nose is cut off and wedged in between the breast plate of your amour and your chest.

亥百必シ死ヘシ右之外ニシテ亀ツクリマト父

キ是ッナラフセ

身裝コホシモノ

是ハ敵ニ亍味方ニ弓箭サカシニシテセンサリ

ツヨキ家々ニ亍ハ宿城ヘトリカケテシ備フイタス

程ニ亍ハ二三度ノセリ合ニ亍ツル亥ハナキモ

ノセ然者押出押込押返勝負ハナリシテ

セリ合ニ三度亍四五度ニ百之刻能武切ノ

勇士備ノ能謀有亍味方ハキシヒ敵方

事有、　必シルベシ、　右之外ニシテ鼻ヲカクコトハ大

キ是ヲキラフ也

身衆コボレモノ

是ハ敵モ味方モ弓箭サカンニシテセンサク

ツヨキ家々ニテハ宿城ヘトリカケラレ備ヲイタス

程ニテハ一二度ノセリ合ニテクツル〻事ハナキモ

ノ也、　然者押出、　押込、　押返、　勝負ハナクシテ

セリ合ニ二三度モ四五度モ有之刻、　能武功ノ

勇士備ノ能　謀　有テ味方ハキヲヒ敵方

右の外に鼻を掻き取る事は、（どんな人間の首を取ったか、また鼻が潰れて変形して切り口と合わない等、判別が困難な事もあって）大いに忌み嫌われるものであります。

身衆こぼれもの

　これは敵も味方も弓矢などの武芸に秀でて戦闘の訓練が行き届き、結束の強い一族郎党は、宿城を敵に攻め寄せられても戦闘体勢を整えて反撃に出るまでの一、二度の小競り合い程度の戦闘で敗退する事はないものです。当然ながら、押し込み、押し出し、押し返しの一進一退の攻防をせず、その場所での合戦が二、三度も四、五度も繰り返されるものであります。

In the end all of what is written above (From whom was the head taken? Has the nose been crushed or been misshapen? Does it fit the head from which it was said to have been cut? And other concerns regarding identification) is anathema to Samurai.

Shin Shu and Kobore Mono

Mass of People and Those That Spill Out??

This type of battle deals directly with the degree of proficiency in the martial art of archery developed by both you and your enemy. When the castle or stronghold of a division with strong unity comes under assault they do not need to reform their fighting ranks in order to launch its first or even its second counter strike. They will remain in place despite one or two small skirmishes. This is because their cohesion has not faltered in the least. It goes without saying that such a unit would not be pushing in, being driven back and then forced away in a back and forth battle. They may join combat in the same spot two, three, four even five times.

ヲ以テ勝貝始ルニ道腸（三ケ敬ルハ大概了

ソハモノ也是ヲコホシ音トヱ能侍ハアメーリテ

退リ必ナリニ是ノ身衆トヱ也縦ハ人ノニ

ウハストモ身衆付ノ手柄トシコホシモノニ

付ノホメサルヲナリヌヲリシタル方ノ侍ニ裴奏

返合或能詞ノツカニ人ノサシ物ナトント

ニテアラハ取テヤ（シヤウニ仕ルハヘリシタル

武士ノ作法アリノコトシ

ヲクレテ勝負始ルニ道脇ヘニゲ散ルハ大概ア

ヲハモノ也、是ヲ、コボレ者ト云、能侍ハカタマリテ

退リ、必打ニクシ、是ヲ身衆ト云也、縦ハ人ヲ

ウタストモ身衆付ヲ手柄トシ、コボレモノニ

付ヲホメザルナリ、又ヲクレタル方ノ侍モ幾度モ

返合、或能詞ヲツカヒ人ノサシ物ナド、ヲト

シテアラバ取テカエルヤウニ仕ルハ、スグレタル

武士ノ作法カクノゴトシ

49

このとき武功に秀でた勇士は、陣営内で謀略を巡らし、味方を勇気づけて敵方の気力を挫くもので、戦いが始まると矢面から幾分安全な道脇に逃げ去るのは、大概が青葉者であります。これをこぼれ者といいます。優れた侍は、一塊になって退却するので、攻撃しづらいものです。これを身衆といいます。たとえ敵を討ち取らなくても身衆付きに攻め掛かる事自体が手柄となり、こぼれ者に攻め掛かる事は褒められません。又、戦いに敗れた場合にも、何度も反撃を試み、※敵に向かい罵詈雑言などの言葉を発して挑発をして敵を混乱させたり、敵の指物などが落ちていれば、拾って帰るのは、優れた武士の合戦作法であります。

※悪口（あっこう）と現代語訳に利用した参考文献にある。

During such an action a Samurai of meritorious service will move about inside the division passing on strategy, encouraging his side and disparaging the opponent, breaking their will. When the fighting begins and the brunt of the impact of your forces fall upon the enemy soldiers some of them will begin to stream away. For the most part it will be Blue Leaf soldiers that will be seeking safe paths. These people are what are known as Kobore Mono, those that spill away. Skilled Samurai will withdraw as a single solid group and is therefore difficult to attack. This is what is known as Shin Shu, or a mass of people(in this case a group of soldiers still in formation). If, for example, you were to attack a Shin Shu you would receive Merit for that action even if you do not succeed in cutting anyone down. Cutting down a Kobore Mono would not result in being awarded merit.

Further, even should your side be defeated if you attempt attacks several times and hurl insults and jibes at the opponent to the degree that the enemy becomes furious and thrown into disarray or you pick up and bring home Yubi-mono, finger decorations, belonging to the enemy know that this is an example of excellent Bushi battle tactics.

雄鑑巻第十八目録

千柄批判

一 下覚之働之亳

一 弱倫批判之亳

一 仇討之亳

一 放討之亳

雄鑑巻第十八目録

手柄批判

一　不覚之働之事
一　弱備批判之事
一　仇討之事
一　放討之事

雄鑑巻第十八目録

手柄批判

ふかくのはたらきのこと
一、不覚之働之事
じゃくびひはんのこと
一、弱備批判之事
あだうちのこと
一、仇討之事
はなしうちのこと
一、放討之事

Yukan Scroll Number Eighteen Table of Contents

A Discussion of Merit

1. How to Work With Surprise and the Unexpected
2. A Discussion of When You are Underprepared
3. On the Topic of Revenge Killing
4. On the Topic of Group Execution

手柄ノ批判 下

一 病首

大合戦ニ人ヲ討ハタシ首帳調テ後證人ニ

一 無之首ヲ取末侍ヲ名付病首取ト名付也

子細ハ敵陳ニテ雑人相順行歩モ不叶ニ辰テ

味方ニ捨ラレカクレテ有ツアルヲ出ニテ頭ヲ捕

人十三ツニモ三ツニトヱル侍ハ膿病ノ仕ル所也

故如此定也但能士カリシ若クルツクハカリ出テ

カラメ取テ来ルハ右ノタクノヒニテラス

手柄ノ批判　下

一　病首

大合戰ニ人ヲ討ハグレ首帳調テ後證人モ

コレナキクビ トリクル
無之首ヲ取來侍ヲ名付病首取ト名付也

子細ハ敵陣ニテ雜人相煩、行歩モ不叶ニ依テ
ゾウニン、アイワズライテ　ギョウホ　不可能　ヨッ

味方ニ捨テラレカクレテ有ヲ探シ出シテ頭ヲ捕
隱　レ　テ　　　　　　　　　　　　　クビ　トリ

人ナミノシルシニセントスル侍ハ臆病者ノ仕ル所也
印

故如此定也、但能士カクレ居タルヲタバカリ出シテ
故ニカクノゴトク定ムナリ　　　　　　　　謀　リ

カラメ取テ來ルハ右ノタグヒニアラズ
類　イ

55

手柄批判下

一　病首

大合戦で敵を討ちそびれて、首帳を調べてから証人もない首を取ってくる侍を名付けて病首取りといいます。なぜならば、敵陣で雑兵などが傷病により歩行さえ不可能となり、味方に見捨てられて隠れているのを探し出して殺して首を取り、それ相当の手柄となる首級に偽装しようとすることは臆病者の所業であります。故に病首取りと、このように定められます。但し、隠れている敗残兵を謀（たばか）って誘い出し、捕縛して来るのは病首の類には該当しません。

Tegara Hihan Shita

Second Part of a Critique of Honor and Merit

One Chapter

Yamai Kubi

Taking the Head of a Sick Person

Upon failing during the course of combat to take the head of an enemy a Samurai brings forth a head that has no corresponding witness entered into the Kubicho, or book recording the heads taken. Such a head will be treated as a "head taken from the sick or lame." The reason for this is that mercenaries and so forth, mixed in with the enemy's forces may have become sick or injured and thus abandoned by their comrades. They may also have been hiding with other members of the defeated side and been flushed out and then cut down. The severed heads are then made to appear as if they are of a vastly higher rank. This is truly the work of a coward.

For that reason it is known as "taking the head of a wick or infirm." That being said, discovering where members of the defeated forces are hiding and drawing them out and doing Hosbaku, or binding them up, is not in any way considered similar to taking of Yamai Kubi as was stated above.

一　女首

右ノコトノ大合戦ナトノ刻證人ナリシテ鼻シ
アキ来ル侍ハ女首取ト名付類也子細ハ其首ノ
善悪見分ラレス圖刀或女坊主ノ首カト疑ノ有力
故ニ能武士ハ仕作法ニテラス是シ女ノ首トルト定也

一　作頭

作頭ト云ハ雑人ノ首ヲ取能シルシニセシト敬之
捨テ敗軍ニナル甲ナトノ有ツヒロヒウキセ首帳ニ
ノセシトスル是作首ト名付ケイハクナルシツ

一 女首

右ノゴトク大合戰ナドノ刻、証人ナクシテ鼻ヲ

カキ来ル侍ハ女首取ト名付類也、子細ハ其首ノ

善悪見分ラレズ、圀（味方）カ 或ハ、女、坊主ノ首カト疑ノ有ガ

故ニ能武士ノ 仕 作法ニアラズ、是ヲ女ノ首トルト定 也

一 作頭

作頭ト云ハ雜人ノ首ヲ取、能シルシニセント敵之

捨テ敗軍シタル甲ナドノ有ヲヒロヒテキセ首帳ニ

ノセントスル、是作首ト名付、ケイハクナルヲク

一　女首

　右（前述の病首）のように大合戦などのとき、証人を付けずに敵の鼻を切り取って来る者は女首取りと呼称されます。なぜなら鼻だけでは、その首が手柄に出来るものか否かの判断がし難く、※味方の首や女や坊主の首かとの疑いがかけられますので武士の行う方法ではありません。故に女首取りと判定されるものです。

※参考文献では、取る事自体に問題があり、取れば重罪として罰せられるとある。

一　作頭（つくりくび）

　作頭（作首）というのは雑兵の首を取り、敗走した敵の兜をかぶらせて武将級の武士の首級に偽装して※首帳に記載させようとすることをさします。これを作首と呼び、軽薄で臆病な武士のすることであります。

※首帳…討ち取った首と其れを取った者の名前を記した首注文ともいう帳簿

One Chapter

Onna Kubi

Woman's Head

As was mentioned above (similar to Yamai Kubi), following a great battle, a Samurai presenting the severed nose of an enemy combatant with no associated witness is referred to as "the taking of a woman's head." The reason for this is that if only the nose is presented it is difficult to ascertain the rank of the person it belonged to. It is after all possible that it could be the nose of a Samurai from your own side, a woman or even from the head of a monk.* As presenting it would bring up such doubts it is not a method a Bushi should make use of. For this reason presenting such a thing is designated as the "taking of a woman's head."

*Other resources indicate that the action of taking the head of such a person if true would result in severe punishment.

One Chapter

Tsukuri Kubi

A Manufactured Head

Manufacturing a head or Tsukuri Kubi, is when you take the head of a rank and file soldier and placing it inside the helmet of a higher ranking soldier who had left it behind when fleeing. Attempting to have such a head entered into the Kubicho*, or record of heads taken in battle is referred to as Tsukuri Kubi. A Bushi doing something like this is shallow and cowardly.

* The Kubicho also contained notations regarding the head and the manner in which it was taken.

ヒヤウノ武士ノ仕ル處也

一 捨首

捨首ト云ハ合戦或ハ小迫合ニテ敵味方ノ間ニ

於テ死タル者多百ツ味方ノ侍敵ノ身衆（ヘ

アリ古ノ千頁无人ニハ目ツモカケス捨テトシ

ルノ其跡ニテ取タルヲ捨首ト云但是ハ武切之

侍ニツハイテヲ歩ノ小者中間十ト□是クトラス不

覚ト云（カヽス是ノ能武士ノイトラス不覚中ナモ□）

一 㓤鑓

一　捨首

捨首ト云ハ大合戰或ハ小迫合ニモ敵味方ノ間ニ

於テ死タル者多有ヲ味方ノ侍、敵ノ身衆へ

カゝリ右ノ手負死人ニハ目ヲモカケス捨テトヲ

ルヲ其跡ニテ取タルヲ捨首ト云也、但是ハ武功之

侍ニツゝイテ歩ノ小者中間ナトノ是ヲトラハ不

覚ト云ベカラズ、是ヲ能武士ノトラバ不覚ノ中ナルベシ

一　狗鑓

ビヤウ武士ノ仕ル処也

一　捨首

　捨首というのは、大合戦や小競り合いでも、敵味方の間で死んだ者が多くいるのを味方の侍が敵の身衆へ攻め掛かっていき、そこに転がっている敵方の死傷者には目もくれずに捨て去るのを、後からくっ付いて行って死傷者の首を取るのを捨首といいます。但し、武功の侍に付<ruby>随<rt>つきしたが</rt></ruby>って歩く※<u>小者中間</u>などが敵方の死傷者の首を取っても不覚(愚かな振舞い)とはいえません。これを武士がやれば不覚に該当します。

一　<ruby>狗鑓<rt>いぬやり</rt></ruby>（犬鎗）

※小者中間…雑務等の奉公に従事する身分の低い者

One Chapter

Sute Kubi

Discarded Head

A Discarded Head is a term used for situations after a large battle or skirmish where many Samurai were felled. The warriors on your side fell upon the enemy Mass of People 身衆. The enemy that fall to your swords are ignored at that time. Going back later and taking the heads of the dead is known as Sute Kubi, or collecting the heads of those you had left (discarded) behind.

That being said a valiant Samurai would be accompanied by by Komono or Chugen, low level workers that take care of general tasks, would be the ones to take the heads of the dead. Doing it is this way is in no way indiscreet (i.e. shameful /cowardly behavior). However a Bushi doing it on his own would be an indiscretion.

One Chapter

Inu Yari

Dog Spear

垣塀或ハ築地ナトヲ隔テ鑓ヲ合又馬上ノ鑓或ハ

敵ヲ追クツシテヨリ後二人三人カゝリメゝリテ退所ニ

追責討ントスレハ敵モ鑓ヲナシスト鑓合スルモ

アレハハ又フサレヒトヒ本ノ鑓トハイハスレケルシ

一番鑓ナトノマウニ思ヒ過言スレヲ 犭鑓ト

名付不覚ト定レ也

弱俗批判

一見崩

見崩ヒト云ハ敵掛來ン見テ勝頭ヲ見ゝナリレテ

66

垣塀 或ハ 筑地ナドヲ隔テ鑓ヲ合、 又ハ馬上ノ鑓、 或ハ

敵ヲ追クツシテヨリ後二人三人カタマリテ退所へ

追責討ントスレバ敵モ鑓ヲナヲスト鑓合スルモ

アシクハアラサレトモ本ノ鑓トハイハス、 シカルヲ

一番鑓ナドノヤウニ思ヒ過言スルヲ狗鑓ト

名付不覚ト定ル也

弱備批判

一 見崩

見崩レト云ハ敵掛來ヲ見テ勝負モナクシテ

67

垣や塀、築地などの遮蔽物に隠れて敵を鎗で突き殺したり、馬で駆け抜けざまに馬上から鎗で突くことをいいます。或は、敵を追い散して、二〜三人の少人数で逃げているところを追撃して、敵も体勢を立て直して反撃に打って出てきて鎗を交えますが、少人数を攻撃するので卑怯とまでいわぬものの、本来の武士の戦い方とはいえません。このような戦い方をして一番鎗等のような功名を得たと勘違いして過言することを犬鎗と名付け、愚かな振舞いであるとされます。

弱備批判

一　見崩

見崩というのは、敵が攻め掛かって来るのを見て、浮足立って戦いを挑みもせず、我先にと退却することを見崩といいます。

68

Striking out at the enemy with a spear whilst remaining undercover behind an obstructing wall, hedgerow or piled up reclaimed land is known as Dog Spear.

In addition, the following also fall under the same category:

- Riding out from behind such a blind and charging the enemy on horseback and impaling them on your spear or
- Scattering the enemy forces and attacking a small group of two or three

If such a group were to turn about, regroup and attack then a Yari-ai, or spear fight would ensue. However attacking such a group while not exactly cowardly would hardly fall into the realm of how Bushi are supposed to fight.

Jakubi Hihan

A Critique of Being Underprepared

One Chapter

Mi-Kuzure

Mi-Kuzure, or breaking on sight, is a term that refers to when the sight of the attacking forces causes the opposing forces to abandon sanding lightly on the balls of their feet ready to fight. Rather, they flee before your vanguard even reaches them. This is called Mi-Kuzure

崩ヲ見崩トヱセ

一　ウラクツし

胴勢二ノ午或ハ後偸ノ裏敵聞ニ見定ス

シラクツルヽ亥百リ　是ヲシソウクツレトヱセ

一　友崩

呼方ノ來ヲ敵カト思リツルヽ亥百是ヲ友崩ト

云右是等ハ軍法ヲシカラサル偸ハ常ニ有ヱ亥也

一　仇討

アリヽキウナ亥チラウ人ハ畫夜トヒニ心馭

崩 ヲ見崩ト云也

一 ウラクツレ

胴勢ニノ手或ハ後備ノ衆、敵間モ見定ズ

シテクツル〻事有リ、是ヲウラクツレト云也

一 友崩

味方ノ來ヲ敵カト思、クツル〻事有、是ヲ友崩ト

云、右是等ハ軍法タ〻シカラサル備ニハ常ニ有ル事也

仇討

一 カタキウチノ事、子ラウ人ハ昼夜トモニ心掛

71

一　うらくずれ（裏崩）

胴勢（軍勢の中間に位置する部隊）、二の手（第二陣、先鋒
部隊に続く部隊）或は、後備（後方守備部隊）の衆（将兵）
が敵軍との距離や戦況の良し悪しを見定めずに状況不利と思
い込み、混乱して退却する事があります。これが裏崩という
ものであります。

一　友崩

味方の部隊が来るのを敵軍が攻めて来たと思い込み、軍勢が
崩れる事があります。これを友崩といいます。見崩や裏崩、
友崩のような事は、軍法（兵法）を間違っていたり、軍事訓
練が不十分な軍勢には、常に発生するものであります。

仇討

一　敵討ちの事、仇討ちをする人は昼夜ともに仇を討ち果た
す事を心掛けて時分に関係なく、仇敵に遭遇したら、時を改
めずに討ち果たすべきで、これを無上の名誉とします。

One Chapter

Ura-Kuzure

Falling Apart from the Rear

This describes a problem with the commander of the midsection (a unit stationed in the middle of a division) a Ni-no-te, second string forces (typically stationed behind the vanguard) or even Bobi, the rear guard. He is unable to determine the distance from and condition of the enemy forces. Thinking that the conditions are unfavorable things get confused and the forces withdraw. This is known as Ura-Kuzure.

One Chapter

Tomo-Kuzure

Falling Apart Due to Aligned Forces

The enemy forces come to believe that an approaching unit is an attacking force and the whole division falls apart. This is referred to as Tomo-Kuzure, or falling into disarray after mistaking friendly forces for enemy forces. These two phenomenon, Mi-Kuzushi and Tomo-Kuzushi frequently occur in divisions that have a mistaken belief of military strategies or have not trained sufficiently.

One Chapter

Adauchi

Revenge Killing

On the subject of revenge killing. It is important to remember that it matters not if it is night or day, if you encounter the person you have a vendetta against you must cut him down. No matter what time or day you meet such a person you should immediately dispatch him. By doing so you will receive an uncountable amount of Merit.

時分ノハカス相逢ノ限ニ考ハタスヘシ時刻ノ移

ス事無之ッ上ス子細ハ時節ノツテヒ月日ノ

送シ間ニ人間生者必滅老少不定ノナラヒ横死

ンセハ本意ノトケスシテヤミヌルノミニテフスノ次

ノ武人ノ嘲ノモツヽ〳〵古人モ云ヲ得ノラハ

本意ノトケ運ツヽヽハ捨身ノ報トスヘシト

申サヒナルセ

子ラハ人ハ常ニ寝屋ソカ〳〵寝食ノヤスノ

セス晝豆夜用心ヲ堅固ニシテ行路ニテ敵ヲ見ハ

時分ヲハカス相逢ヲ限ニ打ハタスヘシ時刻ヲ移

ス事無之ヲ上トス、子細ハ時節ヲウカゝヒ月日ヲ

送ル間ニ人間生者必滅老少不定ノナラヒ横死

ヲセバ本意ヲトケスシテヤミタルノミニアラズ、家

ノ疵人ノ嘲ヲモウクヘシ、古人モ云、打得タラバ

本意ヲトゲ、運ツキナバ捨身ヲ報トスベシト

申サレタル也

子ラハルゝ人ハ常ニ寝屋ヲカヘ寝食ヲヤスク

セズ昼夜用心ヲ堅固ニシテ行路ニモ敵ヲ見バ

詳細を述べますと時節を伺い、月日を送る内に人間、生きていれば必ず年老いて死ぬものであります。仇討ちを達成せずに死去すれば、本懐を遂げずに終わるのみでなく、家の名誉を疵付けた一族の大恥という侮蔑をも受ける事になります。昔の人も仇を討てば、本懐を遂げられるが、武運尽きたら、捨身で立ち向かって仇を討つべきであると仰っております。

仇敵となって狙われる者は、常に寝所を変え、寝食を安易にせずに昼夜、警戒を厳重にして、行路にも仇討ちに来た敵を見付けたら、道を変えて逃れ、討たれないことを手柄とします。

The reason for this being, if you were to wait for a certain time the fact of the matter is that as a human we all age and die as the sun rises and sets and moon goes through its phases. Dying without achieving your long sought after goal of avenging yourself is not only a failure for yourself but can blemish your family's name. This shame can result in scorn and contempt being directed at your family.

People who lived long ago believed that striking down a hated enemy in revenge would allow you to achieve your lifelong dream. Having completed your service in the fortunes of war they say you should throw yourself wholeheartedly into coming face to face with your adversary and strike him down.

A person who is being targeted for revenge should sleep in a different place every night as a matter of course. Meals should not be taken leisurely either at midday nor in the evening. The strictest precautions should be taken. If, while on the road, you encounter an enemy bent on revenge immediately alter your course and escape. Make not being subject to a revenge killing a source of pride.

道ソカ（不討ノ手柄トス血气氣ノ勇者ハ是ン

ソヒルトモ邪義ナレハ聞入（ヘカラス本文云用心ハ

臆病ニシテ心ヲ剛ニ持（ヘシトヱ合戦ヒヨリ合

ヒトノ剣親兄弟ナトシ敵ニウツモ和睦ノ後

ハノキナリ上ヲ遺恨ニヲツモノ百是大成ヒカ支也

子細ハ敵ニ呼方ニ主恩ヲステ身命ツツ

其報謝ノ念イハシリイクヒトノ運ヲ付クタルニ

何ノ恨カフラハ低ヲ能武セヲ丁ハ玉死骸

ヲ送リヒ亡魂ヲトムフフハ弓矢ノ禮ノ義ニモセシヘハ

道ヲカヘ、不討ヲ手柄トス、血氣ノ勇者ハ是ヲ

ソシルトモ邪義ナレバ聞入ベカラズ、本文云用心ヲバ

臆病ニシテ心ヲ剛ニ持ベシト云々、合戰セリ合

ナドノ刻、親兄弟ナドヲ敵ニウタセ和睦ノ後

カタキナリトテ遺恨ニモツモノ有、是大成ヒガ事也

子細ハ敵モ味方モ主恩ヲ以テ身命ヲツナギ

其報謝ノタメハシリメグルトテ運ツキウタレタルニ

何ノ恨ガアラン、去ニ依テ能武士ヲ打テバ其死骸

ヲ送リ亡魂ヲトムラフハ弓矢ノ礼義也、シカレバ

　血気にはやる者にこの事をを恥ずかしい行いであると誹
謗されることもありますが、仇を討ちに来た者から逃れる事
を誹謗^{ひぼう}する事自体が間違いですので聞き入れてはなりません。
仇敵となったら臆病な程に用心しておいて心を剛強に保つべ
きということであります。

　合戦や競り合い等の時に親兄弟等を敵方によって討ち取
られて合戦や競り合い等の和睦^{わぼく}成立後に仇であると敵方の将
兵に対して遺恨を持つ者もおりますが、これは大間違いな事
であります。なぜなら敵も味方も主君に仕え、主恩を以って
身命を繋いでおり、その報恩のために戦場を縦横無尽に駆け
巡って戦い抜き、武運尽きて討ち取られたとして何の恨みが
ありましょうか。更に身分の高い武士を討ち取れば、その遺
体を相手方親族に送って亡魂^{ぼうこん}を弔^{とむら}うことは弓箭^{きゅうせん}の道の礼儀
であります。

Particularly those who are young and full of vigor may feel ashamed at such actions and may resent being slandered about it. Be that as it may, the concept of evading and escaping from the threat of a person seeking to cut you down in revenge is mistaken and should be completely ignored. Being the object of someone's vendetta means that you have to maintain a level of caution usually attributed to an Okubyomono, or coward. Your heart must remain ever strong and vigilant.

In the course of a large battle, or even a small skirmish, it is possible that the enemy forces cut down a relative, parent or brother or yours. If, following that great battle, skirmish or some such a reconciliation is agreed upon then holding a grudge and seeking a vendetta against solders of the opposing side is completely out of line.

The reason for this being that both you and the opposing soldiers serve their respective lords. Your life is tied to the obligations you have to your lord. To honor your commitment to your lord you charged to all corners of the battlefield. Having abandoned yourself to being cut down in whatever way the fates of war see fit, to then emerge unscathed from that what kind of grudge could you possibly have?

Further, should you cut down a Bushi of high standing it is considered proper etiquette for those on the path of war to return the body of your opponent to his family with your condolences for the departed Samurai's soul.

合戦和談ノ後タカイニ出合其報謝アルハ

勇士ノ習成ニ結句恨ヲ継アラメツ報ヒスルハ

能作法ニ不可也此故ニカ亥ナリト定也

放討

一科人百之時其所一即時ニシヨニ、え科人イカホト

アルソトメツナ何道具ノ取持ニテ何力アルト

聞定アフナケモナク、テシ、込ホ取青能武士ノ作法

即時ニシ、云ミ、ワレストテソ、シハヒカ亥也放キノ

青氷ノ内ニテモ廣庭ニテモ切テ出ブメルニ

合戰和談ノ以後タガイニ出合、其報謝アルハ

勇士ノ習成ニ結 勾恨ヲ結、アダヲ報ントスルハ

能作法ニ不有也、此故ニヒガ事ナリト定也

放討

一 科人有之時、其所へ即時ニオシコマズ科人イカホド

アルゾトタツ子 何 道具ヲ取持シテ何方ニアルト

聞定、アブナゲモナクシテヲシ込、打取者、能武士ノ作法也

即時ニオシコミウタストテソシルハヒカ事也、放打ノ

者、家ノ内ニテモ廣庭ニテモ切テ出テタルニ

当然ながら合戦和談成立以降に敵味方に分かれて戦った者同士が互いに行き会った時に、その報謝（死骸を送り亡魂を弔ってもらった事に対しての恩に報い、その徳に感謝して御礼の品物を贈る等をして謝礼する事）をするのが勇士としての仕来たりでありますが、反対に恨みを募らせて仇を討たんとするのは、人に誇れる振る舞い方と言えるでしょうか？　それゆえに和議成立後の仇討ちは、道理に反することと定まります。

放し討

一　討ち取りの対象となった科人（とがにん）が居るとき、その居場所に即座に押し込まず、科人の人数を調べあげ、所持している武器の種類や居場所を特定し、大きな危険を冒さずに相手方の居場所に踏み込んで、科人を討ち取る者は、有能な武士のやり方であります。即時に踏み込んで討ち取らぬ事を誇る事は、大間違いであります。屋敷内でも玄関先の庭から土間においても、科人が斬って出てきたところに真っ先に掛って行って最初に科人と切り結んだ者の手柄となります。

It goes without saying that following the successful joining of a peace treaty, former allies and enemies that fought each other would then go their separate ways. They may well encounter one another during the course of conducting such courtesies (In return for the respect shown by having the body of a fallen relative returned to be prayed over, acknowledging the act of deference and repaying that virtuous act by sending a gift of some sort) which are after all a custom of Bushi. If however one side were to allow their grudge to fester into anger and then become enraged and cut the other person down in revenge, would this then be classified as the type of behavior to bring honor to a person? For this very reason following the successful joining of a peace treaty revenge killings are classified as being contrary to reason.

One Chapter

Hanashi Uchi

Group Execution

A criminal who is to be executed should not be immediately cut down then and there. You should first determine how many accomplices he has, investigate the number and type of weapons he possesses as well as his whereabouts. All this should be established first. Without putting yourself in undue danger got to the place his accomplices are said to be.

The criminal should be executed by a very experienced Bushi. To criticize the action of not cutting down a criminal immediately is a great error.

Even should a sword wielding Toganin, or criminal, burst in through the main gate and into the enclosed garden around the main buildings or the cleared earth before the house the first person to charge straight in and achieve a cut on the bandit achieves Merit.

最前ニアリテ切結タル人ハ手柄也如斯剣腸

アラテ後カラモ別人ヨリテ此科人ヲ切フセタリ

トモ一ノ手柄ハ初ノ人ナルヘシ子細ハ二人勝負少

争所ナ勿ヨリヨッテハ切ヨ故也然ハ最前ニ

切結タル人科ニ切殺サレテ其セニサリシ如

此後ノ人ガシトメタリトモタヒニトレ所ハチヨヤ

エ(七但スイワニ初ニアリテ切結タリニ善者ノ

テ留スニテ後ノ人ニヨリテ走退ハ不覚トええ也

敷討ノ到科人勝員ゼスニテ足ハヤニ逃行シ

最前ニカ丶リテ切結（キリムスビ）タル人、手柄也、如斯（カクノゴトキトキ）刻脇

カラモ後カラモ別人ヨリテ此科人ヲ切フセタリ

トモ一ノ手柄ハ初ノ人ナルベシ、子細ハ二人勝負ヲ

争（アラソウ）所ヲ脇ヨリヨツテ（寄ッテ）ハ切ヨキ故也、縦ハ最前ニ

切結タル人科人ニ切殺サル丶ト云トモ其センサクハ（穿鑿）如

此（ノ如シ）、後ノ人シトメタリトモ（仕留メ）、クタビレタル（草臥レ）所ハ打ヨキ（討チョキ）

故（故シ）也、但又イカニ（但シ）初ニカ丶リテ切結タリモ其者ヲ（討チ止メズ）

ユヘ也、後ノ人ニユツリテ立退ハ不覚ト定也（サダムルナリ）

打留ズシテ（譲リ）（ハジメ）（ニゲユク）

放討ノ刻科人勝負セズシテ足ハヤニ逃行ヲ

86

この時に、その脇や後ろから別の者が接近して科人を斬り伏せたとしても一番の手柄は、最初に斬りかかった者のものになります。なぜなら二人で戦っているところを脇から寄って斬れば、簡単に斬り伏せられるからです。たとえ最前に切り結んだ者が罪人に斬り殺されたとしても一番の手柄は最初に切り結んだ者の手柄となります。後から来た者が罪人を仕留めたとしても、疲労しているところに斬りかかったのでは、討ち取りやすいからです。但し、如何に真っ先に斬りかかって切り結んだとしても、罪人を仕留めず、後から来た者に手柄を譲って立ち退くのは、愚かな事と定められます。

放し討の時、科人が一戦も交えずに足早に逃げて行ってしまったときに、科人を討ち取らなかったと謗る者がいます。

The reason for this is that whilst two people are fighting it is relatively simple to move in from the side and cut the criminal down. For example, even if a person at the front of the fight cuts the criminal down, he will not receive as much Merit as the person that made the first cut. While other Samurai may run up and join combat, even finishing off the criminal he has been exhausted by the previous cut and is thus an easy kill.

If you are the first to engage and cut the criminal but do not succeed in killing him, you should be aware that allowing the Merit for the kill to pass to a person who came up later and cut him down to be an act of cowardice.

Should a Toganin, or criminal, who has entered the grounds of a compound not engage anyone but rapidly flee without being cut down, there will be some that are critical of this.

キシトメメトテソシル人有是ツソシルモ無理也

足ハヤミケテ追ツカレスハイカンカセンス被官ナシ

切トテ手負ル人ツソシル者有不案内成

家風ノ取サメセ子細ハ小者中間ナリトモワシ

サシ脇指ツサシメル者カ心ケナケテヌキ合勝ツ貝シ

ヒハ其時ノ仕合ニテ手負ニモナトカナカフシ然ルシ

其場ノ様子モキカスニテ無理ニツシモニカ亥也

右之條々者近代之良将之所ン被置足其匡

也後ノ人順如斯手柄穿鑿可被定者也

打トメヌトテソシル人有、是ヲソシルモ無理也

足バヤニニゲテ追イツカレズバイカンセン又被官ナドヲ

切トテ手負タル人ヲソシル者有、不案内成

家風ノ取ザタ也、子細ハ小者中間ナリトモ刀ヲ

サシ脇指ヲサシタル者ガ心ケナゲニテヌキ合勝負ヲ

セバ其時ノ仕合ニテ手負事モナドカナラン、然ルヲ

其場ノ様子モキカズシテ無理ニソシルモヒガ事也

右之條々者近代之良将之所以被置定其区

也、後ノ人慎如斯手柄穿鑿可被定者也

これを謗るのは、無茶苦茶な事であります。科人の足が速い時、科人が全速力で逃げているのを追走して追い付くのは非常に困難であり、追い付けなければ、どうしようもありません。

又、被官などを斬ったときに、負傷した者を謗る者がいますが、兵法の知識や心得がなくて、放討の様子や事情を理解していない兵法に疎い者（うといもの）の個人的見解にすぎません。なぜなら、小者や中間であっても刀を差し、脇指を差した者が勇猛果敢に抜刀して戦えば、「窮鼠かえって猫を噛む」という言葉の通り、必死の抵抗となり、その時の戦いで放し討に向かった武士が負傷する事も致し方のないことです。それにも拘らず、その場の様子も見聞せずに無理に謗るのは大間違いであります。

右の各条項は、その区分毎に定められることで、近代の良将であるという事の根拠とされます。後の人は慎んで（つつしん）このような手柄詮索（てがらせんさく）は評定されるに任せるべきであります。

90

This criticism is wildly out of place. If the Toganin is fleet of foot and is going full out in his retreat overcoming his speed and striking him down is extremely difficult. If he cannot be caught then he cannot be caught.

In addition there are those that would criticize a Bushi that was wounded in the process of cutting down a Hikan, or low level Samurai (often attached to a higher level Samurai). Such a person's knowledge and wisdom regarding military strategy are clearly flawed. The opinion of a person who has but a meager knowledge of military strategy and possesses no understanding of the place and circumstances of the incident can be dismissed out of hand. The reason for this is that though the opponent may be a Komono, a footman, or Chugen, a mid-level servant, they still have a blade in their belt. Upon drawing their Wakizashi, short sword, such a person could fight with dauntless courage, much like the saying about a cornered rat turning and ferociously attacking the cat that was staking it.

There really is no blame to be laid upon a Bushi who receives an injury in the course of being the first fighter in a Hoshi Uchi, or group execution. It can't be helped. The criticism of a person who completely ignores all of that and doesn't take into account the situation on the ground is completely wrong.

All of the conditions detailed in the chapters above have been established to serve as fundamentals for the great generals of today. I trust that those that follow will evaluate and judge with humility situations where Merit is to be awarded.

雄鑑第十九目録

　　出軍

一　出軍門出之作法

一　傭押之作法

一　同行列之次第

　　出軍

　　出軍門出之作法

一　夫出陳ノ作法ハ先大将出方ニ終テ白言方作

雄鑑第十九目録

　　出軍

一　出軍門出之作法

一　備押之作法

一　同行列之次第

　　　　出軍

　　出軍門出之作法

一　夫出陳ノ作法ハ先大将出立終テ向吉方乍
　　　　　　　　　ソレ出陣　　　　マズ、大将シュッタツオエ　　キッポウヲムキナガラ

雄鑑第十九目録

　　出軍

一　出軍門出之作法
　しゅつぐんかででのさほう

一　備押之作法
　びおうのさほう

一　同行列之次第
　どうこうぎょうれつのしだい

　　　　出軍

　　出軍門出之作法

一　そもそも出陣の作法は、先ず大将は出立の準備を終えて、吉方に向けながら、扇子を持って※左の足を上にして八文字形にして座られます。

※床几等に座るが低ければ、左足を前に胡坐のように足を組んで座り、床几が高ければ右足を前に出して足を大きく拡げて座る。

立ち上がって、一歩踏み出すときに左足から踏み出すことが、しきたりとなっているので、胡坐のように座したちきは、左足が前でなければ右足から踏み出すこととなり、両足を拡げて座っていたときは、右足が予め前に出ていれば、自然と左足から最初の一歩を踏み出せる。

Paragon of Military Strategy

Chapter Nineteen Table of Contents

Departing for War

One Chapter

Etiquette for Departing Through the Main Gat

One Chapter

Etiquette While Completing Preparations

One Chapter

Pertaining to the Chapter Above: Forming the Ranks

One Chapter

Shutsugun

Departing for War

Etiquette for Departing Through the Main Gate

From long ago the proper etiquette for a departing unit begins first with the Taisho, or general, having finished his preparations. The Taisho then, holding his Sensu folding fan and facing a favorable direction sits (onto his camp stool). He sits more or less cross-legged with his left leg on top and his legs making Hachimonji, the shape of the Kanji eight 八.

※ If the stool or chair is fairly low then the left foot goes out front as if you were going to sit down cross legged. If it is a tall chair then the right leg should be slightly forward with legs opened wide. When standing, etiquette dictates you should step out with the left foot. If sitting cross legged and your left leg is not forward then you would end up stepping out with the right first. If you are seated with both legs wide open and the right leg is slightly forward, then the first step would naturally be with the left.

持扇たる足ヲ上ミシテ八文字秋座シ玉フ時

御祝之肴酒ヲ参スヘシ御肴ハ舟鮑同カ子クリ也

是ツ二種ノ肴ト乵又三種ノ肴ト云ハ右ノ二種

ノ肴ニ昆布ヲ加テ三種ノ肴ト云也可調様ハ

常ノ人ハ舟鮑一節二節ツリ為大将人ハ舟鮑ツ

シリ也下三四上三五四堅五横ニシク之是九字ツ

ヒヤウシ故也次ニ勝栗三ツ行ムツ、置ニカメ

勝ト云心也昆布ハ大キニ切テ一切也此肴ヲ調ヲ

又ニ子ノ人ニ不可見可秘ト云 口傳

96

持扇之足ヲ上ニシテ八文字形 ニ座シ玉フ時

御祝之肴酒ヲ参スヘシ、御肴ハ打蚫、同カチクリ也

是ヲ二種ノ肴ト云也、又三種ノ肴ト云ハ右ノ二種

ノ肴ニ昆布ヲ加テ三種ノ肴ト云也、可調様ハ

常ノ人ハ打蚫一筋二筋ヲク、為大将人ハ打蚫九ツ

ヲク也、下ニ四、上ニ五、四竪五横ニヲクヘシ、是九字ヲ

ヒヤウスル故也、次ニ勝栗三ツ片々ツヽ置、ミカタ

勝ト云心也、昆布ハ大キニ切テ一切也、此肴ヲ調ル事

アマ子ク人ニ不可見可秘ト云、口傳

97

そこに御給仕役が御祝いの肴酒を持参する事になります。御肴は打蚫、同じく勝栗であり、これを二種の肴といいます。又、三種の肴ともうしますと、先程の二種の肴に昆布を加えて三種の肴といいます。

　この肴の用意の仕方は、一般の武士は、打蚫を一筋か二筋を皿に置きますが、大将と見做される武士は、打蚫を皿に九本置くのであります。更に打蚫を下に四本、上に五本重ねて、四本を縦向きに五本を横向き並べて置き、この形で九字（早九字）を表します。次に勝栗三つを皿の片側ずつにそれぞれ置いて味方が勝つという験を担ぎます。昆布は大きく切って一切れにします。この肴の用意は、携わる者以外の者には見せてはならず、秘密裏に行うべきものです。口伝

八文字形に座し給うとき……
……左足より踏み出し……
左足から踏み出す為に、丈のある腰掛けに座る時、左足を少し引いて座ると立ち上がる時に、自然に右足に重心がかかり、左足から踏み出せる。
胡坐の時は、左足を前にする。

八　左足を少し引くと丁度、八の字となる。

From there the person who has been designated to bring the celebratory appetizers called, Sakana, and the Sake then presents them. One appetizer should be pounded dried abalone and the other candied chestnuts. Having only two items is known as a two variety appetizer. Further, if an appetizer of three items is to be presented then Konbu seaweed would be added to aforementioned double appetizer. This would be a triple variety appetizer.

The way this appetizer is to be prepared is as follows: For a Bushi of average standing, one or two slices of pounded Abalone would be arranged on a plate, however to be suitable for a General with the rank of general, nine slices of pounded Abalone should be arranged on the plate. Further, four strips of pounded Abalone are laid below with five strips laid above. The four strips are vertical with the five strips laid down horizontally. This shape depicts the Kuji, Next three Kachi Kuri, or winning chestnuts, are placed one by one near the edge of the dish. These possess the effect of allowing your side to win. The Konbu seaweed should be cut into one large piece. When preparing these appetizers it is essential that they be kept hidden from view from anyone other than the person preparing the appetizers. There is a Kuden, or oral transmission, regarding this.

Illustrated Note:

Left: Seated with the feet in Hachimonji.

Right: The left foot in front

When seating yourself in Hachimonji, you should first step out with the left foot. The reason you step out with the left is that in order to seat yourself strongly the left foot is pulled back slightly. Then, when you stand up, your body weight will naturally be on the right foot. Then step out with the left foot. When seated cross-legged the left leg should be in front.

By pulling your left foot back slightly your feet make the Kanji for eight 八.

一右之肴大将食シタラハ残ハ扨炮ヨリ食シ扨

勝栗ヲ食シ玉フ扨勝ト云也此

肴ヲ祝セ其時ハ扨炮長キヤラフ用テ勝ノ

悦ト進セ三種ノ肴ッハ扨勝喜ノ勝悦ト食シ

タレラヘヒト云也

一御給仕ノ作法ハ役者三人百御酌取一人提

一人瓶子一人セ先瓶子ニ酒ヲ入持ヌ奉軍神ニ

其酒ヲ御前ニテ則銚子ヘ可移始中終シマル

足ノフムヘカラス是ハ酌取之秘支物見ニテモ

一 右之肴大将食シタマフヘキ様ハ、打蚫ヨリ食シ、扨

勝栗ヲ食シ玉フ、打勝ト云心也、但飯陳之砌モ此

肴ヲ祝也、其時ハ打蚫長キナカラ用テ、勝ノシ

悦ト進也、三種ノ肴ヲバ打勝喜、ノシ勝悦ト食シ

タマフヘシト云也

一 御給仕ノ作法ハ役者三人有、御酌取一人、提

一人瓶子一人也、先瓶子ニ酒ノ入持テ奉軍神ニ、

其酒ヲ御前ニテ則銚子ヘ可移、始中終シサル

足ヲフムヘカラス、是酌取之秘事、物具ニテモ

一　右の肴を大将が召し上がる順番は、打蚫から食べ、次に勝栗を召し上がって頂き、戦いに打ち勝つという心を表します。また、凱陣式の時もこの肴で祝いますが、その時は、打蚫は長いままで用意して勝栗、熨斗鮑、悦ぶ（昆布）「敵に勝ち（栗）、家（うち＝打蚫）ながく、よろこぶ（昆布）」の順となります。

出陣式では三種の肴を打ち勝つ喜ぶ、熨斗て勝つ悦ぶ（昆布）の順に召し上がるべきと申します。

一　御給仕の作法は、御給仕役に

御酌取の役が一人、

提で酒の補充に当たる役が一人、

瓶子の役が一人

の合計三人就きます。まず瓶子に酒を入れて持ち、軍神に奉納して、その御酒を大将の御前で御酌取役の持つ長柄の銚子へと移します。※出陣式の開始より終了まで、後退りをしてはなりません。これは、御酌取の秘事であり、物具の扱いに於いても物具の上げ下げの時にも蹲踞の姿勢で行わなければなりません。

※参考文献より…後退は、合戦での敗退や退却を連想させる為。御酒を注ぎ足すときは、左に方回りして提役の所に向う。

One Chapter

The order in which the appetizers listed above are eaten by the general is as follows. First the pounded Abalone is eaten, then he should consume the Kachi Kuri, boiled chestnuts, which express the spirit of striking the opponent down and winning. In addition, when celebrating the triumphal return of a unit these same appetizers are eaten That being said, at that time the pounded Abalone is left as one long pounded strip. The order they are consumed is first chestnuts, then abalone and then seaweed. A play on words makes the order of eating sound something akin to "We won against our enemy (with our winning chestnuts) and our house (which pounded the enemy flat like the Abalone) will grant us pleasure for a long time as will this seaweed (the word for this type of seaweed, Konbu, sounds like the word for pleasure yorokobu). This is the order of eating. When departing for battle the triple appetizer should be eaten in an order that reflects the sense of Pound! Win! Joy! The Pound! of Abalone, the "Win!" of chestnuts and the "Joy" of seaweed.

One Chapter

The etiquette for those waiting upon the Shogun is as follows. Those serving as honorable attendants are the pourer of Sake, the distributor of Sake (who fills the Choshi decanter with Sake from the Hisage, a bucket with handle and spout) and the handler of the Choshi decanter. There are a total of three in all. First of all the Sake is poured into the Choshi and it is taken up, offered to the Gunshin, or God of War. Next, in the presence of the General, that sake is transferred into a long handled Choshi decanter by the honorable pourer. Throughout this departure ceremony you should never allow yourself to move backwards (Other resources indicated that backing up was the equivalent to withdrawing from a battle. When pouring the Sake you should revolve counter-clockwise). This is a secret teaching for those honored with serving the Sake. When you are moving the utensils and objects for this

上下ニテモツノハイ可取タノチノ釼ニツクリテ

腰ニ納右ノ手ハカリニテ可取手ツツ叓十カレ

サテ可参ヲ様ハ三三九度也一献三度完三度

加ルハ九字ヲ表スル故サテ御タノカメ〔ヨルヽ〕

大將ハ音ノ右之方ヘ出シテツレ無心ニシテ心ヲ

不動タノ足ヨリフミ出シテサニ七足ノ

ニハイーシフムヽシテ足ノヘニハイト云八

貪巨録文篆武破ヲノ八ノ八ーセ

口傳者之圖

104

上下ニテモ蹲踞（ツクバイ）可取、左ノ手ヲ剣ニツクリテ

腰ニ納、右ノ手ハカリニテ可取、手ヲツク事ナカレ

サテ可参様ハ三三九度也、一献ニ二度宛三度

加ルハ九字ヲ表スル故也、サテ御左ノカタヘヨルベシ

大将ハ肴ヲ右之方ヘ出シナヲシ、無心ニシテ心ヲ

不動、左ノ足ヨリフミ出シ立サマニ七足ノ

ヘンバイヲフムベシ、七足ノヘンバイト云ハ

貪巨録文簾武破ノヘンバイ也

口傳者之圖

105

左手を剣を表す形にして腰にあてて右手のみで物具を取り扱わなければなりません。また※１床に手をついてはなりません。そして御酌の行い方は、三三九度（三献の儀）であります。一献につき、二度ずつ細く注ぎ、三度目を太く長く加えるのは、（三献につき三度御酌する為、三×三で九。即ち三三九度）九字を表現するためであります。さらに出陣式では全動作を左側から行わなければなりません。三献の儀の後、大将は御肴（折敷や高坏）を右側に除けてから心を静めて保ち、左足から踏み出して立ち上がりざまに七足の反閇を踏むのであります。※２七足の反閇とは、貪巨録彣簾武破の七字の反閇であります。

口伝はこの図の通りです。（次頁の図）

※１、参考文献に手や膝を着く事は、忌み嫌われるとある。

※２、一般的な九字の「臨兵闘者皆陣列在前」と同様の呪文結印に該当する北条流兵法独特の呪文結印と推測されます。

Henbai Dance
貪-Don＝Desire
巨-Kyo＝Gigantic
録-Roku＝Record
彣-Chi＝Following after
簾-Ren＝ Bamboo mat
武-Bu＝ Military
破-Ha＝ Break

Kuji
臨　Rin - Power
兵　Pyo - Energy
闘　Toh - Harmony
者　Sha - Healing
皆　Kai - Intuition
陣　Jin -Awareness
列　Retsu -Dimension
在　Zai - Creation
前　Zen - Absolute

You must keep your left hand should be on your hip as if holding a sword while you move the implements around. Further, it is absolutely forbidden for you to put your hand on the ground (In addition other research materials indicate that it is detestable to place the knees or hands on the ground).

The way the blessed Sake is to be poured is known as San San Kyudo (Also referred to as Sanken no Gi, the three offerings). Each time you pour you should pour a thin stream twice then, for the third pour, allow the Sake to flow in a long, thick stream. (The three cups are filled with three pours each meaning 3 X 3=9. A three times three equals nine times. This is the meaning of San San Kyudo.) This represents the Kuji. In addition all of the movements done for the departure ceremony must be from the left side.

Following the ritual of the three pours, the lacquered tray that held the appetizers is removed from the General's right. He should then calm his spirit. Then, moving his left foot out he should stand up and do the seven steps of the Hanbai, a ceremonial magic dance done by a general to protect his unit. The seven steps of the Hanbai are the Hanbai of the following seven Kanji.

The Kuden is as shown in the illustration.

Note: For the Hanbai Dance neither the way the Kanji are read nor their overall meaning is given. It appears that within Hojo Military Science this Hanbai (left chart, previous page) is a mystical binding and chant spell that serves the same purpose as the more common Kuji (right chart, previous page.)

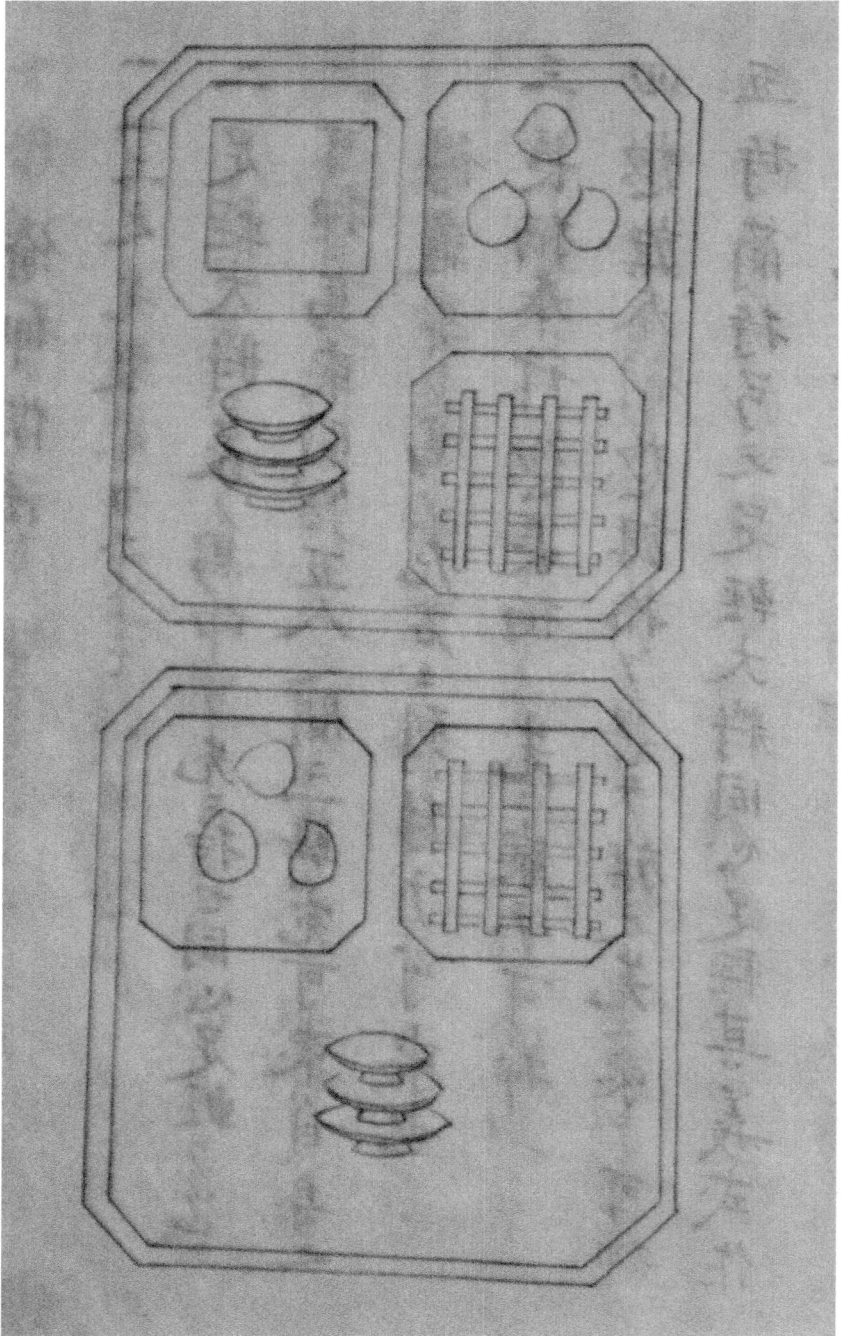

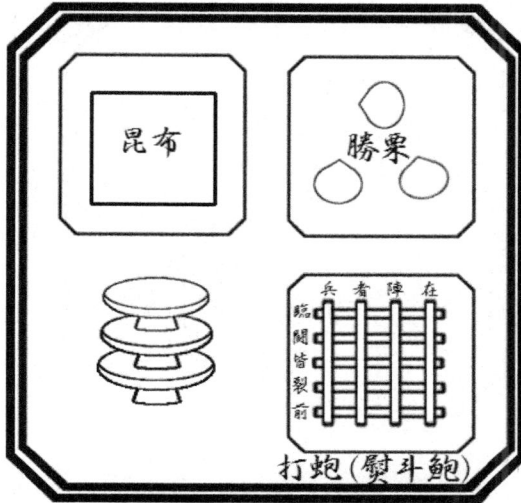

・昆布を大きく一切れにて、大いに喜ぶ。または、喜んで人
(敵)を斬れの意味と推測出来る。
・勝栗を三方に置いて、味方が合戦に勝つの意で勝ち栗。
・打ち蚫を九字の形に並べて、最前で勇猛果敢に打ち(討ち)
合う。

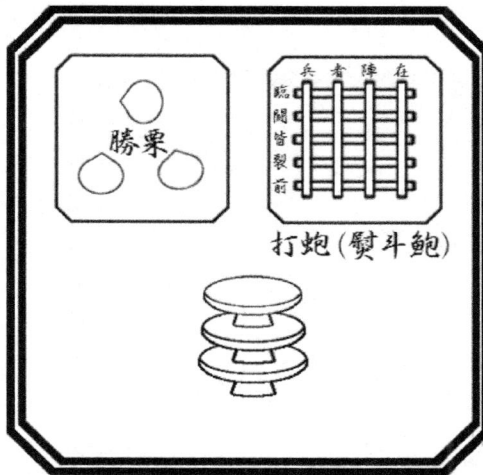

・勝栗を三方に置いて、味方が合戦に勝つの意で勝ち栗。
・打ち蚫を九字の形に並べて、最前で勇猛果敢に打ち(討ち)
合う。

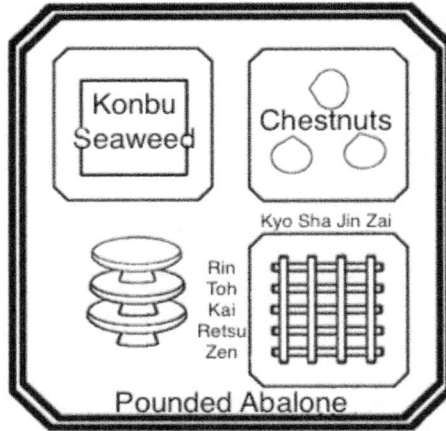

- The Konbu will be cut into one large piece with the meaning of large happiness. Also happily cutting down my enemies could also be construed.
- Placing the winning chestnuts on the Sanpo serving table means that my compatriots and I will win.
- The pounded Abalone is formed in the pattern of the Kuji granting me powerful bravery to pound down my enemies.

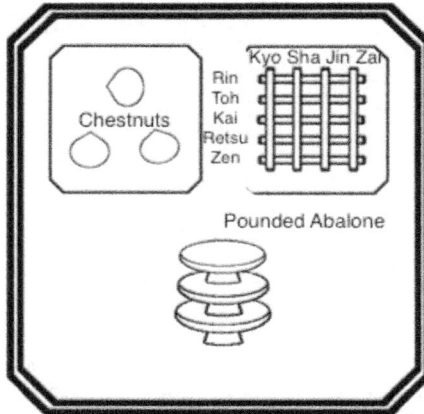

- Placing the winning chestnuts on the Sanpo serving table means that my compatriots and I will win.
- The pounded Abalone is formed in the pattern of the Kuji granting me powerful bravery to pound down my enemies.

傗押作法

一二之先衆イカホトモ

二 足輕大將家ノ馬卬ン先ニ持セ同心足輕ッッレ
可押馬來同心八五人之間三騎宛可來自身之
得道具ッ馬ノ左右ニ引付テ可來也

三 長柄奉行惣長柄ノ先ニ乘テ可押

四 惣旗奉行惣旗指ッッレテ旗之先ニ乘テ可押

五 持簡持弓之足輕大將同心足輕其ニ義式作
法八御先足輕ニッナシ

備押作法（ビオウサホウ）

一　一二之先衆イカホドモ

二　足軽大将、家ノ馬印ヲ先ニ持セ、同心足軽ヲツレテ可押、馬乗同心ハ五人之間ニ一騎宛可乗、自身之

三　得道具ヲ馬ノ左右ニ引付テ可乗也

四　長柄奉行、惣長柄ノ先ニ乗テ可押
惣旗奉行、惣旗指ヲツレテ旗之先ニ乗テ可押

五　持筒持弓之足軽大将、同心、足軽、其義式作
法ハ御先足軽ニオナジ

112

備押作法

一　第一陣と第二陣の先行部隊の人数は問いません。

二　足軽大将は、馬印を先行の足軽に持たせて同心や足軽を率いて進軍。馬乗同心は足軽五名の間を一騎ずつ進み、使う武器を足軽に持たせて馬の左右を行かせます。

三　長柄奉行は、長柄足軽隊の先頭を騎馬で進みます。

四　総奉行は、旗奉行が指揮監督する旗差を引き連れて、旗差隊の先頭を騎馬で進軍します。

五　持筒（鉄砲持）、持弓の足軽大将、同心、足軽の進軍の作法は先行する足軽組と同じであります。

Bi-o Saho

Etiquette During Preparations

One

Do not ask how many men are in the vanguard of the first and second units. (Possibly meaning it doesn't matter how many)

Two

The Ashigaru "Lightfoot" Taisho, or general over the low level foot soldiers, has an Ashigaru soldier at the front carry his Umajirushi, or battle standard of command as they proceed forward with the Doshin, troops one rank higher than Lightfoot soldiers. A Doshin mounted on horseback will proceed between every group of five Lightfoot soldiers. They will hold his weapons as they march on the left and right.

Three

The Samurai magistrate in charge of long weapons will proceed on horseback in front of the long weapon armed Lightfoot soldiers.

Four

The supervising magistrate proceeds on horseback ahead of the Hatasashi Magistrate and the Hatasashi units under his command. (Hatasashi are soldiers with flags mounted on their backs)

Five

The etiquette for the way the Taisho of the Ashigaru armed with matchlocks or armed with bows proceeds and the Doshin is the same as for the other Ashigaru units.

六 御持鑓奉行二騎御持鑓之左右ノ先ニ乘テ可押

七 御旗奉行二騎御旗ノ跡先ニ乘可押

八 御使武者我ラノ得道具ヲ馬ノ左右ニ引付テ
可乘又右ノ内ヲテ半分御大將ノ御後ニサシ
續テ来是ハ御跡へ御用ノタメナリ

九 武者奉行二騎是ハ壽番ハ右ニ乘偷ノ下知
ス非番ハ左ニ乘テ敵ヨリノ方ヘ物見ニ出テ
ハシラリヘヽマウスヲ見ハカ兄セ

十 歩行之侍御大將ノ御前ノ二可歩目付掃目ノ

六

御持鑓奉行、二騎御持鑓之左右ノ先ニ乗テ可押

御持鑓奉行　二騎御持鑓ノ左右ノ先ニ乗テ押スベシ

七

御旗奉行二騎御旗ノ跡先ニ乗可押

御旗奉行　二騎御旗ノ後先ニ乗リ押スベシ

八

御使武者我々ノ得道具ヲ馬ノ左右ニ引付テ可乗、又右ノ内ニテ半分、御大将ノ御後ニサシ

御使武者我々ノ得道具ヲ馬ノ左右ニ引キ付ケテ乗ルベシ　マタ右ノ内ニテ半分　御大将ノ御後ニサシ

九

続テ乗、是ハ御跡ヘノ御用ノタメナリ

武者奉行二騎、是ハ当番ハ右ニ乗、備ノ下知ヲナス、非番ハ左ニ乗テ敵チカツカハ物見ニ出テハタラクベキヤウスヲ見ハカル也

続テ乗リ　コレハ御後

武者奉行二騎　コレハ当番ハ右ニ乗　備ノ下知ヲ　為ス　非番ハ左ニ乗テ敵近付カバ物見ニ出テ　働クベキ様子ヲ見ハカルナリ

十

歩行之侍、御大将ノ御前ヲ可歩、目付横目ノ

歩行ノ侍　御大将ノ御前ヲ歩クベシ　目付横日ノ

116

六　御持鑓奉行二騎は、鑓持足軽隊の左右先頭を騎馬にて進軍します。

七　旗奉行二騎は、旗差隊の前後を騎馬で進軍します。

八　御使武者は、我が軍の使用する武器を持たせた足軽を馬の左右に配置して騎馬で進軍します。また御使い武者の半数は、総大将の後方に続いて騎馬で進軍して、総大将からの用事を後方部隊に伝達する為に備えます。

九　武者奉行二騎。当番の者は、行列の右側を騎馬にて進み、全部隊の指揮命令に当たります。非番の者は、左側を騎馬で進み、敵地に近づいたら、偵察に出て状況を判断するのであります。

十　歩行の侍は、総大将の前方を徒歩で進軍します。

Six

The two mounted magistrates armed with spears proceed on horseback to the font right and left of the Ashigaru armed with spears.

Seven

Two mounted magistrates in charge of the Hatasashi flag bearers, proceed on horseback one in front and one behind the Hatasashi unit.

Eight

Honorable messenger warriors proceed on horseback and are given weapons that match those of your own forces. Ashigaru soldiers are placed to the left and right of their horses. Further, approximately half of the messenger warriors should be on horseback behind the overall commander as he proceeds. These individuals are then ready to transmit orders from the overall commander to the units stationed in the rear.

Nine

There should be two warrior magistrates on horseback. The one who is "on duty" rides along the right side of the unit on his mount and gives orders to all the units in the army. The other one is "off duty" and he rides his mount along the left side and as the army approaches enemy territory goes out and observes to determine the conditions that lay ahead.

Ten

Samurai who are on foot proceed ahead of the overall commander.

侍ハ六奉行ニテニハリ二騎ホト可押其次ニ御歩

行頭ハ御跡ニ乗ルセ其次ニ御中間頭御小人頭

御褒美ノ道具ヲカツアセ可押

十 御小人御中間御馬ノ跡ヲ可歩ノ右ノ内ニテ

番代リニ御馬ノ先ニテ押太皷キ貝ヲ吹ナリ

是御小人ノ役也キ様ハ武者奉行是ヨ

下知ハ御先御跡ハ御旗末ヲ守ラヰセ但百口傳

十二ニヨリ足軽大将名ル〔ニ〕行列 御先足軽ニツ〔シ〕

十三 御陳ニ随兵御腸ニ御後ニヨリ偹イカホトヒ

侍ハ六奉行ニマジハリ一二騎程ホド可押、其次ニ御歩

行頭ハ御跡ニ乗ル也、其次ニ御中間頭、御小人頭、

御褒美ノ道具ヲカツガセ可押

十一

御小人御中間御馬ノ跡ヲ可歩、右ノ内ニテ

番代リニ御馬ノ先ニテ押、太鼓打、貝ヲ吹ナリ、

是御小人ノ役也、打様ハ武者奉行是ヲ

十二

下知ス、御先御跡ハ御旗本ヲ守テ打也、但有口伝

シマリ足軽大将タルベシ、行列御先足軽ニオナジ

十三

御陳ニ随兵、御脇一二御後シマリノ備イカホドモ

目付や横目の役職の侍は、六奉行に交わって一、二騎ほどで進軍します。後方を進む歩行頭は、総大将の後方にて騎馬で進軍します。更にその後方で中間頭、小人頭が中間や小人に褒美の品々を入れた長持等を担がせて進みます。

十一　小人、中間は、総大将の馬の後を歩きます。その中から番代りに総大将の馬の前で太鼓を打ったり法螺貝を吹く役に就くのであります。これは小人の役割であって太鼓の打ち方等は、武者奉行が指示を出します。前進するのが後進するのかは、武者奉行の居る旗本隊から目を離さずに太鼓を打ちます。その詳細は口伝です。

十二　行列最後尾の守備は、足軽大将が務めます。行列の編成は、先行部隊の足軽組と同じです。

十三　行列に随伴する兵は、脇備に一〜二隊、最後尾に随伴する兵を大多数続かせて進軍すべきであります。

The Samurai that are serving as Metsuke or Yokome, two kinds of investigators, change out every six stations and consists of two or more mounted riders. The head of the Samurai walking to the rear is on horseback behind the overall commander. Further the heads of the Chukan, the mid ranked servants, and the Shonin, the lowest ranked servants, have the Nagamochi oblong chests and so on filled with various gifts.

Eleven

Shonin and Chukan walk behind the overall commander. Members of this group take turns walking in front of the overall commander's horse and beat a Taiko drum or blow the conch shell trumpet known as a Horagai. This is mainly the job of the Shonin. The way in which the drum is beaten will be directed by the Musha or Samurai Magistrate. Whether proceeding forward or moving back the person with the drum must never take his eyes off where the Musha Magistrate and his vassals are is. Details regarding this are told in Kuden oral transmissions.

Twelve

It falls to the Taisho of the Ashigaru, or the commander of the Lightfoot soldiers, to protect the rear of the army. The arrangement of that unit is the same as the makeup of the Ashigaru unit of the vanguard.

Thirteen

Soldiers accompanying the unit should be arranged so that you proceed with one to two units on each side and the majority forming a rear guard.

寸續テノ入ヘ也

古小荷駄奉行偏先當番跡非番也小荷駄ヲ

中ニシテ可押當番ハ先ニシ小荷駄ヲ守護シ

非番ハ御陳ハラヒシテ出ル故ニ小荷駄ノ

跡ヲ可押ト云也

十五 小荷駄故地ニテハ跡退時ハ先ヘ押也各口傳

行列作法

打続テヲスヘシ
_{打続テ押スベシ}

十四　小荷駄奉行、備先當番、跡非番也、小荷駄ヲ
_{備ノ先ハ、当番}　_{アトハ、ヒバンナリ}

中ニシテ可押、當番ハ先ニヲシ小荷駄ヲ守護シ、
_{押スベシ}　_{押シ}

非番ハ御陳ハラヒヲシテ出ル故ニ小荷駄ノ
_{オ陣払イヲシテイツルユエニ小荷駄ノ}

跡ヲ可押ト云也
_{後ヲ押スベシトイウナリ}

十五　小荷駄、敵地ニテハ跡、退時ハ先ヘ押也、各口傳
_後　_{退ク時}　_{オスナリ}

行列作法

十四　小荷駄奉行は、小荷駄隊の前方を当番が進み、後方は
非番の者が進のであります。当番は、小荷駄隊の先頭を進軍
して小荷駄を守護し、非番は、陣払いをし行列を外れる為、
小荷駄隊の後から進軍するということであります。

十五　小荷駄隊は、敵地では後方を進み、退却時には先頭を
行かせます。　　　　　　　　　　　　各項目に口伝あり

行列作法…行列の編成方法

Fourteen

　　The magistrate in charge of the Konita Porters, a unit made up
of people that carry food, gunpowder and supplies, marches in front
of them. This person is "on duty" while the person who marches at
the end is "off duty." The person on duty is in the front of the
Konide porters and is charged with guarding the provisions. The
person who is off duty at the rear of the provisions column leads the
unit away while the other units are repelling enemy divisions. In
other words the magistrate at the back of the unit becomes the
leaders.

Fifteen

　　Konita Porters proceed from the rear into enemy territory.
When withdrawing they proceed from the front.

There are Kuden for each of these chapters.

The word Saho or etiquette in this chapter means "the way it is to be
done."

御先

一番一二之先衆 イカホトモ
足
二番御足軽
先
三番御長柄

一番一二之先衆 イカホトモ
足
二番御足軽
先
三番御長柄

御先

一番一二之先衆イカホドモ　足
二番御足軽　先
三番御長柄

一番一二之先衆イカホドモ　足
二番御足軽　先
三番御長柄

御先

一番二二之先衆イカホトモ

一番二二之先衆イカホトモ

行列前方に配置された警戒・偵察の任務にあたる部隊。一番は先鋒第一陣、二番は第二陣

足

足

先

先

二番御足軽

二番御足軽

三番御長柄

三番御長柄

足軽大将（騎馬）
先…馬印を持った足軽で馬のやや前を歩く。

長柄奉行

Front of the Division

First Unit
First
and
Second
Forward
Units

Number
not
specified

In the front of the column a unit comprised of guards and scouts will be placed. In first position will be the first of the vanguard units. In second position will be the second vanguard unit.

First Unit
First
and
Second
Forward
Units

Number
not
specified

Ashigaru

Forward

Second
Ashigaru

General of the Ashigaru (Mounted on Horseback) In front: Ashigaru with Umajirushi walks sightly ahead

Ashigaru

Forward

Second
Ashigaru

Third
Long
Weapons

Long weapon magistrate

Third
Long
Weapons

四番惣旗

五番御持足軽

六番御持鑓

七番御使武者

四番惣旗

五番御持足軽

六番御持鑓

七番御使武者

四番惣旗

五番御持足軽

六番御持鑓

七番御使武者

四番惣旗

五番御持足軽

六番御持鑓

七番御使武者

四番惣旗

五番御持足軽

六番御持鑓

七番御使武者

惣奉行
旗奉行

弓鉄砲組足軽隊
足軽大将、同心足軽

御持鑓奉行二騎並び
に主君の鑓持ち役の
隊列。

伝令に当たる武者。

四番惣旗

五番御持足軽

六番御持鑓

七番御使武者

Fourth Position	All Magistrates Flag Magistrate	Fourth Position
All Flags		All Flags

Fifth Position	Ashigaru Units armed with Bow or Matchlock. Ashigaru General. Doshin Ashigaru	Fifth Position
Ashigaru with Arms		Ashigaru with Arms

Sixth Position	Two Magistrates with Spears are Riding Horses Side by Side. The Spear Division for the Lord.	Sixth Position
Soldiers with Spears		Soldiers with Spears

Seventh Position	Musha that receive orders/ messages	Seventh Position
Messengers		Messengers

目付 横目 武者奉行 貝 目付

横目 歩 歩 歩行近習 御使武者

歩 歩 御大将

目付 横目 武者奉行 大鼓 目付

横目 歩 歩 歩行近習 御使武者

目付横目　武者奉行　太皷　目付　横目 歩歩　歩行近習　御使武者

歩

御大将

目付横目　武者奉行　貝　目付　横目 歩歩　歩行近習　御使武者

軍目付

軍令の下知に当たる。

物見(偵察・斥候)に出る。

目付横目　武者奉行

目付横目　武者奉行

貝

貝所役、法螺貝を吹く。

太鼓

太鼓所役、武者奉行の指示で太鼓を打つ。

目付　横目

目付　横目

歩　歩　歩　歩　歩

御大将

歩行近習　御使武者

歩行近習　御使武者

歩…歩行の侍

歩行近習…総大将の身の回りの世話や秘書的な仕事や雑務に従事する。

136

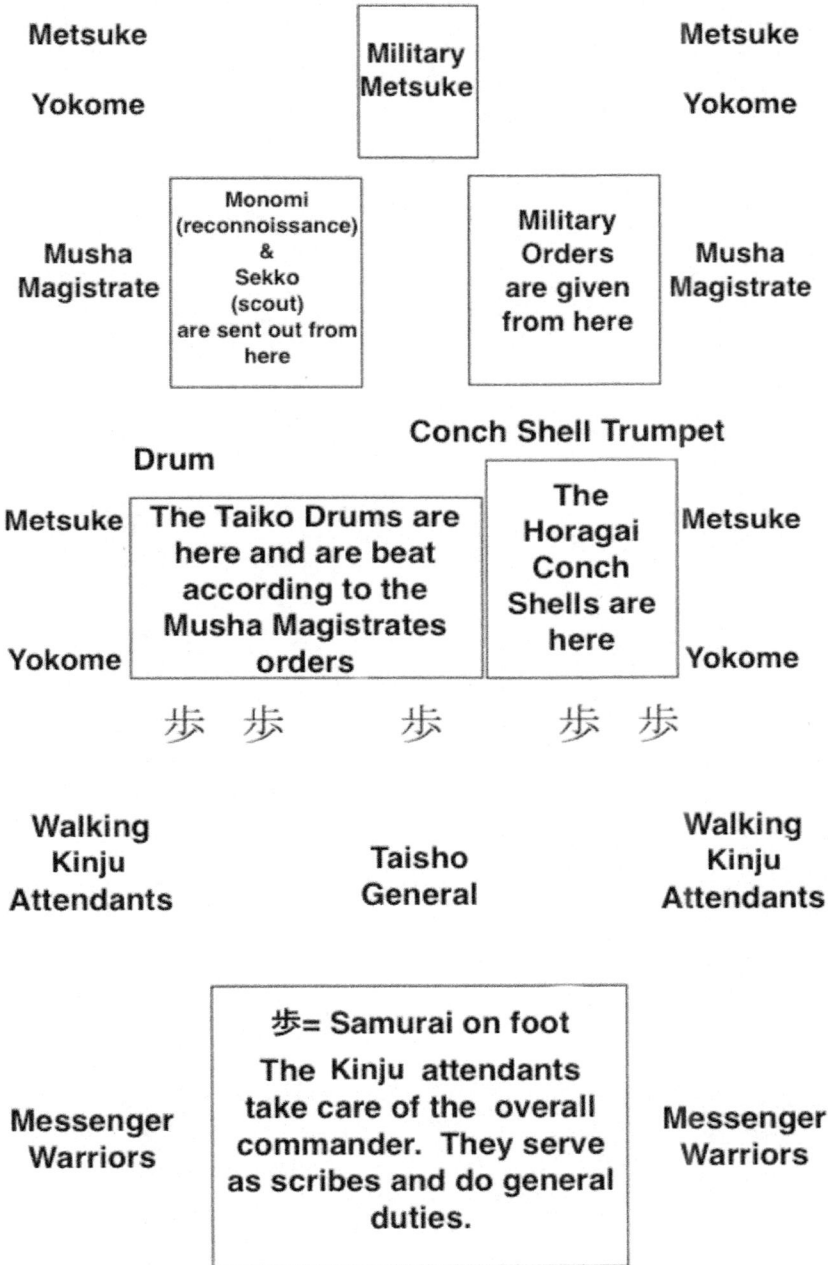

Metsuke

Yokome

Military
Metsuke

Metsuke

Yokome

Musha
Magistrate

Monomi
(reconnoissance)
&
Sekko
(scout)
are sent out from
here

Military
Orders
are given
from here

Musha
Magistrate

Conch Shell Trumpet

Drum

Metsuke

The Taiko Drums are
here and are beat
according to the
Musha Magistrates
orders

The
Horagai
Conch
Shells are
here

Metsuke

Yokome

Yokome

歩　歩　　歩　　歩　歩

Walking
Kinju
Attendants

Taisho
General

Walking
Kinju
Attendants

Messenger
Warriors

歩= Samurai on foot

The Kinju attendants
take care of the overall
commander. They serve
as scribes and do general
duties.

Messenger
Warriors

歩行頭　御小児姓近習　敺足軽

歩行頭　御小児姓近習　敺足軽

陰　陽　脇備

陰　陽　脇備

こゝり後備

こゝり後備

于明中間小者御鎧美入長持

歩行頭　御小兒姓近習　殿足軽　陰陽　脇備　シマリ　後備

手明　中間　小者　御褒美入長持

歩行頭　御小兒姓近習　殿足軽　陰陽　脇備　シマリ　後備

歩行頭　御小児姓近習　殿足軽　陰陽　脇備　シマリ後備

元服前の近習。総大将の身の回りの世話や秘書のような仕事や雑務をこなす。将来、良い武将になる。

将

殿足軽…隊列最後尾を固める足軽大将

手明中間小者御褒美入長持（中間頭、小者頭が褒美の物品を中間や小者に担がせて進軍）

手明…旗差の左右で旗の紐を持ち、旗差の補助をする。
てあき

歩行頭　御小児姓近習　殿足軽　陰陽　脇備　シマリ後備

医者又は陰陽師

脇備、シマリ後備…多数の随伴兵

Head of
Foot
Soldiers

Young
Kinju
Attendants

Shingari
Ashigaru

Head
Lightfoot
Soldiers

Onmyo
Sorcerer

Auxiliary
Troops
for the
Sides
&
"Closing
Troops"

Nagamochi, or
long chest, filled
with gifts being
carried by Tetomo,
Chugen and
Komono.
The head of the
Chugen and head
of the Kobito have
the Chugen and
Kobito under their
command carry
the Nagmochi as
they march.

Doctor or
Sorcerer

The Side
Troops and
the Closing
Troops are
groups of
mercenaries

Kinju that have
not had their
coming of age
ceremony. They
attend to the
overall
commander and
act as scribes
and run
errands. In the
future they will
be good
warriors

Shingari
Ashigaru- The
General of the
Ashigaru who
keeps the end
of the division
in line.

Head of
Foot
Soldiers

Young
Kinju
Attendants

Shingari
Ashigaru

Head
Lightfoot
Soldiers

Onmyo
Sorcerer

Auxiliary
Troops
for the
Sides
&
"Closing
Troops"

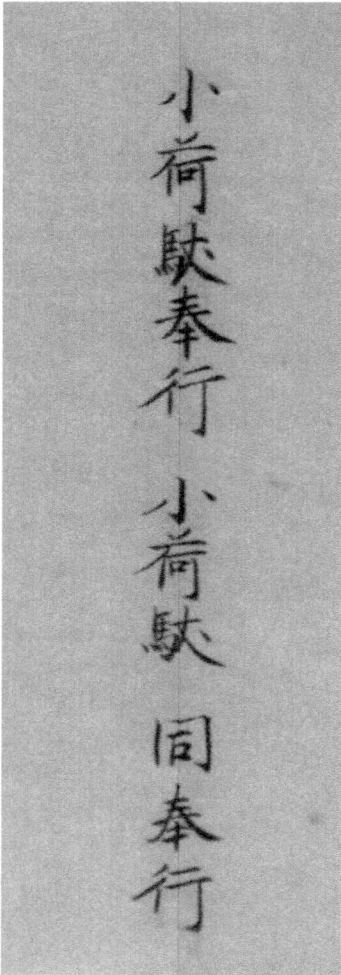

小荷駄奉行　小荷駄　同奉行

小荷駄奉行

当番の小荷
駄奉行。
小荷駄隊の
警護に当た
る。

小荷駄

荷駄隊。
武器弾薬、食料
等の補給物資
を荷駄馬に載
せて運ぶ。

同奉行

非番の小荷
駄奉行

Small Goods Magistrate- The "on duty" Small Goods Magistrate. In charge of guarding the Small Goods Unit.

Small Goods Unit- Weapons, gunpowder, food and other such supplies and materials which are loaded onto horses for transport.

Small Goods Magistrate- This is the "off duty" Small Goods Magistrate.

兵法雄鑑巻第二十目録

戦地

一 敵地働入山ヨリ取寄其德七ヶ條之支

一 山中ヨリ押入作法三ヶ條之支

一 敵地初テ見ル山中ニテ道リアテ人數ヲ通シ

一 先ニノツカ（又ツカ一・ヒ〔ン知支

一 地形變十四ヶ條之支

一 地訳名十五ヶ條之支

兵法雄鑑巻第二十目録

戰地

一　敵地ニ働キ入リ　山寄　ヨリ取寄スルソノトク七ヶ条ノ事
　　敵地働入、山ヨセヨリ取寄其徳七ヶ條之事

一　山中ヨリ押シ入ル作法三ヶ条ノ事
　　山中ヨリ押入作法三ヶ條之事

一　敵地初テ見ル山中ニテ道ヲアテ人数ヲ通シ
　　先ニテツカヘ又ツカヘマジキヲ知事
　　サキニテ間エ又間エマジキヲ知ル事

一　地形變十四ヶ条ノ事
　　地形変十四ヶ條之事

一　地形名十五ヶ条ノ事
　　地形名十五ヶ條之事

145

兵法雄鑑巻第二十目録

　　　戦地

一　敵地に攻め込むときに山寄より攻め込む事及び、その利
益七ヶ條之大事について

一　山中から攻め込む方法、三ヶ条の事について

一　敵地で初めて入る不慣れな山中で迂闊^{うかつ}に通路を決めて多
数の軍勢を進めたときに道の先で味方が閊えてしまう事。又、
自軍がその道の先で閊えてはならない事を知らなくてはなら
ない事について

一　地形変十四ヶ条の事について

一　地形名十五ヶ条の事について

The Paragon of Military Strategy

Volume Twenty

Table of Contents

Senchi

Battleground

One Chapter

When attacking enemy territory you should launch your assault from the mountainside. In addition, twenty reasons as to why this is beneficial.

One Chapter

Three chapters on how to launch attacks in the mountains.

One Chapter

When first entering a mountainous area you are not familiar with do not carelessly commit to a road. Lending numerous troops down that way mans that your own men will be obstructing the way. Further, it is essential to understand that you should never allow your men to obstruct the path ahead of you.

One Chapter

Fourteen Sections on variation in terrain.

One Chapter

Fifteen Sections on terminology for terrain.

戦地

　敵地働入ハ六山寄ヨリ取寄ハ其徳七ヶ條之支

一　小勢ツ以大軍ニ力フモ其手立多シ

二　負軍之時引取ミモ其使有リ

三　敵地戦ナヒトモ険難ヲ越テハ夜軍不叶吏

四　俄ニ城地取タツモテ其徳多シ

五　合戦ノ吉山ヲ呼方ヘ告或ハ我国ヘノ支ヲ聞
　　又加勢ヲヨフ（キ三モ其自由多シ）

六　陳具ツトルニ三モ竹木多シテ味方ニハ其ノ利ヲ

戰地

敵地働入ニハ山寄ヨリ取寄ベシ其德七ヶ條之事

一　小勢ヲ以、大軍ニムカフ（向カウ）モ其手立多シ

二　負軍之時引取ニモ其便有リ（タヨリ）

三　敵地戰ナレドモ險難ヲ越テハ夜軍不叶事（不可能ナ事）

四　俄ニ城地取タツル（立）ニモ其德多シ

五　合戰ノ吉凶ヲ味方ヘ告（ツゲ）、或ハ我国ヘノ事ヲ聞

　　又加勢ヲヨブ（呼ブ）ベキニモ其自由多シ

六　陳具（陣具）ヲトル（取ル）ニモ竹木多シテ味方ニハ其利ヲ

149

戦地

　敵地に攻め込むには、山寄から攻め込むべきである事と、その利益の七ヶ条の事について

一　小勢で大軍を相手に戦う時も、その戦法は多い。

二　敗戦時に退却する際にも良い方法がある。

三　敵地戦であっても険難な所を越えてしまうと夜戦が不可能になる事。

四　突発的に敵の城地を占領するのも利益が多い。

五　合戦の有利不利を味方に報告したり、自国への情報を得る。

又、加勢を要請しなければならない時も、自由が利くほどに手立てが多いものです。

六　陣地を構築する時も、そこに生えている竹木が多く茂っているのを利用すれば味方に有利となり、敵には不利となる事。

Battleground

When advancing to attack enemy held territory you should attack from the mountainside. Seven reasons for why this is the best course of action.

One

There are many military stratagem involving small forces attacking large armies in such a situation.

Two

It is a good method to use in the event of defeat or withdrawing your forces.

Three

Even when battling in the enemy's territory it would be impossible for them to cross over a dangerous sections at night and then attack you.

Four

Launching a sudden violent attack on the enemy's castle and surrounding lands in order to occupy them can bring many rewards.

Five

In the midst of combat you can report on the good or bad tide of battle to your side and that report can be sent on to your Domain. Further, In the event that you have to call for re-enforcements you will not only be free to do so but you can also place them at will.

Six

When building a camp making use of tangled growths of bamboo or trees will be beneficial to your side but hinder the enemy forces.

得敵方其利ノ矢コ支

七　山ヨセヨリ取ヨスレハ　敵國之地下人大ニナツセ

如比徳多クシテ其損スキ故ニ敵國ニ取寄ルニハ

平陸ハ戦ノ好ム處ナリ其國ノ山ヨセヨリ

三　先取敵ヘシト云也故ニ兵法曰　山林以

少勢平衆トマ

山中ヨリ押入作法三ヶ條之支

一　甲列女坂柏坂トトノマウ成難所ハタト八

日本國ニ三ツ二ツノ難所ニレハア複十九

得、敵方其利ヲ失フ事

七

山ヨセヨリ取ヨスレバ敵國之地下人大ニサタツ也
寄　　　　　　　　ジゲニン　　騒立ッ

如此德多クシテ其損ナキ故ニ敵國ヘ取寄ルニハ
此ノ如キ得多クシテ　　　　　　　　　取寄スル　ニ　ハ

平陸ノ戰ヲ好ム事ナク其國ノ山ヨセヨリ
ヘイリク

先取敷ベシト云也、故　　兵法曰　山林以
マズトリシク　　　　　　ユエ　兵法ニ日ク　山林ヲ以テ

少擊衆ト云々
少ガ衆ヲ擊ット云ヌヌ

山中ヨリ押入作法三ヶ條之事
　　　押シ入ル作法

一

甲州女坂柏坂ナドノヤウ成難所ハ、タトヘバ
　　　　　　　　　　　　縦

日本國ニモ一ツニ二ツノ難所ナレバ、カ様ナル
　　　　　　　　　　　　　斯様

153

七　山寄より攻め込めば、敵國の昇殿の勅許のない官吏が
大騒ぎを起こすものです。このように利便性が高く、損では
ありませんので、敵國に攻め込むには、平地での戦いを望ま
ず、その国の山寄から先に攻撃に執りかかるべきといわれま
す。兵法の言葉に、山林を利用すれば小勢が大軍を撃破する
事も可能とあります。

　　山中より攻め込む方法三ヶ条の事

一　甲州の女坂や柏坂などのような難所は、日本でも一二
と言われる難所でありますので、このような悪所を越えて行
くような事をやってはなりません。

Seven

If you attack from the mountains the people of the lowest social order will be thrown into a panic.

There are many benefits to this manner of attack and few weaknesses. When attacking another domain it is said that you should not seek to fight on even ground, but rather seek to engage the enemy coming from the mountainside of that country. In the words of past strategists, if you make good use of mountains and forests it is possible for a small force can crush a great army.

Three Sections on How to Launch Attacks in the Mountains.

One

It is said areas such as the Onna Saka, Woman's Slope of Koshu and Kashiwa Saka, Oak Slope, are number one and two in difficulty in Japan. You should never consider attempting to cross one of these difficult areas.

悪所ッハ不可越行支

二東美濃トトノコトノナル山中ッハ忍ヒッ用テ

先ッ見キリ道ッハアケ山ノ頂々ニ偹ン

立ヘキ支

三十里ノ道ッ十日ニモ押セ一偹完先一進テ

山ノ頂々ニ偹ッ立本道ッハ小荷駄或ハ

雑人ッ通シテ能手配シテ少ノ宛ハ入ヘキ支

悪所ヲバ不可越行事

　コエユクベカラザルコト

二　東美濃ナドノゴトクナル山中ヲハ忍ビヲ用テ

先ヲ見キリ道ヲバアケ、山ノ頂々ニ備ヲ

立ベキ事

三　十里ノ道ヲ十日ニモ押セ一備宛先ヘ進テ

　　　　　　　　　　　　ズツ

山ノ頂　々ニ備ヲ立、本道ヲハ小荷駄或ハ

イタダキイタダキ　タテ

雑人ヲ通シテ能手配シテ少宛ハミ入ベキ事

ヨクテハイ　ズツ食ミ入ルベキ

157

二　東美濃などのような山中では、忍者を偵察に行かせて、行先の情報を十分に得てから通路を決め、山頂毎に陣地を構築する事です。

三　十里の道を十日間にも押し進め、一軍ずつ先へ進めて、山頂毎に陣地を構築します。本道は、小荷駄あるいは、雑人を行かせて、よく準備を整えて事です。

Two

For mountainous areas like the ones in Higashi Mino, present day central Japan, Shinobi, or Ninja, should be sent ahead to scout out the area. Only after obtaining sufficient information should you decide on a road and make camp upon cresting each mountain.

Three

You can cover a route ten Ri in length in ten days. To do so you need to send one division at a time and make camp at the top of each mountain. Divisions of porters and or Zonin, low level servants, should be sent ahead on the main road to prepare.

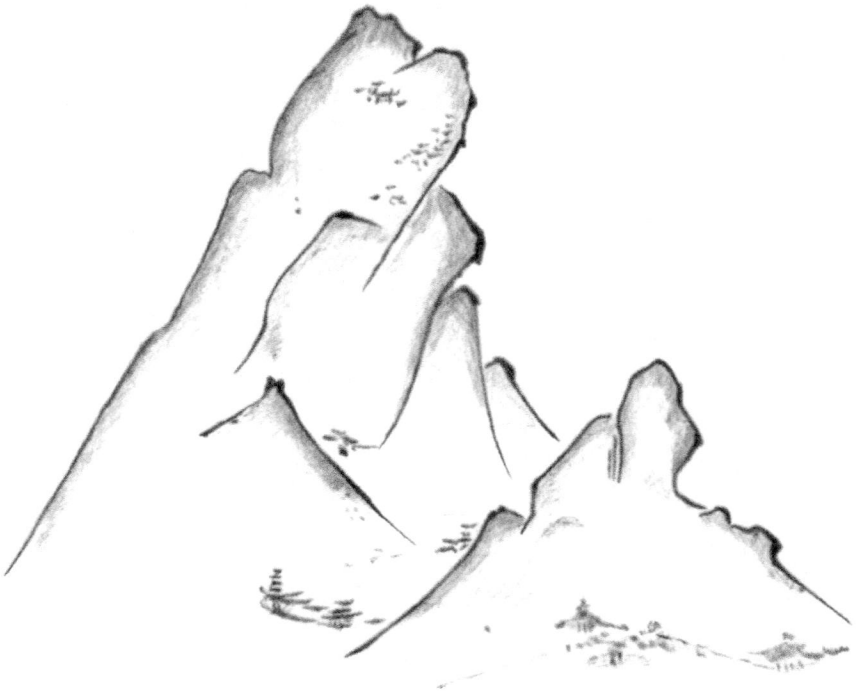

敵地ヲ初テ見セ山中ニテ道ラシテ人数ヲ

通ニ先ニヤツカ（ツカ（ニ）ヒツ知足

一 敵地ハ初テ見セニ山中ナリトセ木性ノ山ヽ東

ヨリアルル将ハノホル所ヨリムワノ方ハ平

或ルヘシト知テ路ヲ當テ人数ノ通スヘシ

一

敵地ヲ初テ見ル山中ニテ道ヲアテ人数ヲ

通シ、先ニテツカへ、ツカへマジキヲ知事

敵地初テ見ルニ山中ナリトモ木性ノ山ヲ東

ヨリアカル時ハノホル所ヨリムカフノ方ハ平

成ルベシト知テ路ヲ當テ人数ヲ通スベシ

162

初めて入る敵地の山中で軍勢を多数進めると道の先で閊えて<ruby>閊<rt>つかえて</rt></ruby>て
しまう事と閊えてはならない事と知る事

一　敵地で初めて入る山中であっても、木性の山を東から登
る時は、登り口より向うはなだらかであろうと判断して通路
を決め、軍勢を多数進めるべきです。

When first entering the enemy's territory from the mountains, if
many troops attempt to proceed forward at the same time the end of
the roadway will quickly become clogged. You should know that you
should not allow this to happen.

One Chapter

Even if this is your first time to enter a particular mountainous
area, if it is a heavily forested mountain and you are climbing from
the east, choose to begin up the mountain at a place that seems to be
more gently sloping. By doing this a greater number of your army
can proceed at the same time.

先ニテツカ立ヒ戔不可者又西ヨリアカル時ハ

此方ヨリムカフハ方ハ険阻成ニヒ卜可知餘者

一 皆是ニテ可知

山之性向東為金姓向南為水姓向西為木姓

向北為火姓向巳未辰戌為土姓其ニ荊平

後険也云々

地形之愛十四ヶ條戔

一 敵味方共ニ往来自由ニ四方ニサワル所ナキシ

通卜云通ノ形ハ先高陽ニ居テ粮道ヲ

一

先ニテツカユル事不可有、又西ヨリアカル時ハ

此方ヨリムカフノ方ハ險阻成ベシト可知、餘者

皆是ニテ可知

山之性向東為金姓、向南為水姓、向西為木姓

向北為火姓、向丑未辰戌為土姓、其前平

後險也云々

地形之変十四ヶ條事

敵味方共ニ徃來自由ニメ四方ニサワル所ナキヲ

通ト云、通ノ形ハ先高陽ニ居テ　粮道ヲ

先で問える事はまずありません。又、西から登る時は此方より向う側は、険阻であろうと判断できます。残る内容はこれで判断できます。

山の性質は、※東に向くと金性となり、南に向くと水性となり、西に向くと木性となり、北に向くと火性となります。丑（北東）、未（南西）、辰（南東）、戌（北西）に向くと土性となります。その前方が平なら、後方は険阻と判断されます。

※山頂の位置がその山のどの方角に寄っているかを示す。

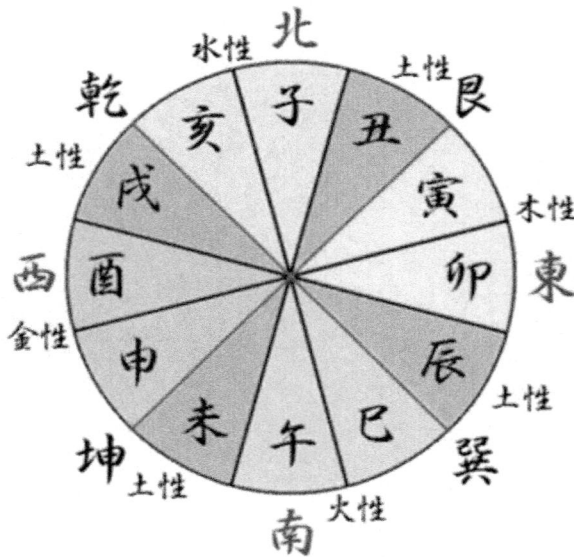

参考図

地形之變十四ヶ條事

一　敵味方共に往来が自由で四方に障害となる所の無い地形を通（つう）といいます。

By doing this there is no chance of your troops getting jammed up. Further, if you are advancing from the west you can determine that the other side is very treacherous. Everything else can be determined from this.

The makeup of the mountain is as follows (if you are on top of the mountain). If looking at it to the east then it is metal in nature. To the south it is water in nature. Looking to the west it is tree in nature and looking to the north it is fire in nature. Ushi, sign of the cow, a combination of north and east, Hitsuji, or sheep, a combination of south and west, Tatsu, a combination of south and east, Inu, or dog, a combination of north and west, would all be earth in nature. From this you can determine that if the land in front of you is even, the land behind it will be treacherous.

Fourteen Sections on Variations in Terrain

One

Terrain that offers free passage with no obstructions in all compass directions for both you and the enemy is known as Tsu, or free passage.

利シムテ戦トキハ則利百トテ云

二 敵味方共ニ出ル支ハヤスケレトモ敵コトノ成難
所有是ヲ拭ト云拭ノ敵ハ敵ニ倍ナケレハ
出テ勝若倍アレハ出テ不勝シテ敵リカタ
ケレハ利アラストテ云

三 我出テモ利アラス敵出テモ利アラサレモノ
地形有如此ナル地形ツ支ト云支ノ形ハ敵
戦ノ利ストイトモ我出ル支ナラ引テ是ヲ
去ル敵ノシテ半出サレメテ是ヲシテハ利アリテ云

二

利シ以テ戰トキハ則利有ト云々

敵味方共ニ出ル事ハヤスケレトモ飯コトノ成難

所有、是ヲ掛ト云掛ノ形ハ敵ニ備ナケレハ

出テ勝、若備アレハ出テ不勝以テ飯リカタ

ケレハ利アラスト云々

三

我出テモ利アラス、敵出テモ利アラサルノ

地形有、如此ナル地形ヲ支ト云、支ノ形ハ敵

我ヲ利ストイエトモ我出ル事ナク引テ是ヲ

去レ敵ヲシテ半出サシメテ是ヲウテハ利アリ云々

通の地形では、先に視界良好で後方への連絡も容易な高地を敵より先に占領し、利用すれば戦況が有利になります。

二　敵味方共に前進して戦うことは容易いが、退却が困難な地形があります。この地形を掛といいます。掛の地形では、敵に備えがなければ、此方から攻めて勝てますが、もし敵に備えがある時には、攻め込んでも勝てないばかりか、退却も困難となって不利益となります。

三　我が軍が出撃しても敵が出撃して来ても共に不利な地形があり、このような地形を支といいます。

支の地形では、敵よりも優勢であってもそこに出撃することなくその場を退き、敵の出撃を誘い、出撃、進軍しているところを撃てば戦況が有利となります。

For areas that are "free passage" you need to take control of the higher ground with a better viewpoint and unobstructed passage behind you before the enemy does. By doing this your prospects in battle will be better.

Two

There are conditions where both your forces as well as the enemy's forces can advance towards each other easily, but withdrawing would prove problematic. This type of ground is known as Kake, or attach. When engaging on Kake Terrain you should finish preparations and attack first. By doing so your side will likely win the confrontation, however if the enemy finishes preparations first and attacks not only are you unlikely to achieve victory but withdrawing will also be difficult. A tough spot to be in.

Three

There is a type of terrain that no matter who attacks first, your side or the enemy, neither has an advantage. This type of ground is known as Shi, or Branched (as in there are many diverging roads/paths cutting across it).

If you are on Branched Terrain and the enemy attacks from a superior position, you can elect not to attack but to withdraw. By decisively drawing the opponent's attack, launching your own attack or advancing you can make this terrain work to your advantage.

* All the readings for the types of land in this section are our best guess. There are also multiple possible meanings for the same type of land.

四 両方山ノ間谷中道馬ニテ人モ多ク立双ニテ
出シ入亥カナヒカタキ地形百是ン隘ト云隘ノ
形ハ我先居之必盈之以待敵若シ敵先居
之盈者勿従ミタサレハ従之云

五 其山ケハシクシテ亦谷深ノ堅固ノ地百如斯
ナレハ険ト云険形者我先居之必居高陽以
待敵モシ敵先居ハ引去之勿従云

六 敵圍深働入味方ノ國地ヲ離ル亥甚遠シ如此
ナレン遠地ト名付テ進テ不可戦之地形ト云也

四

両方山ノ間、谷ノ中道、馬モ人モ多ク立双ンテ

出シ入事カナヒカタキ地形有、是ヲ隘ト云、隘ノ

形ハ我先居之、必盈之以待敵、若シ敵先居

五

之盈者勿從、ミタサレハ從之云々

其山ケハシクシテ亦谷深ク堅固ノ地有、如斯

ナルヲ險ト云、險形者我先居之必居高陽以

待敵、モシ敵先居之ハ引去之勿從云々

六

敵國深働入、味方之國地ヲ離ル事甚遠シ、如此

ナルヲ遠地ト名付テ進テ不可戦之地形ト云也

四　両方が山の間や谷の中の通路で人馬が横並びで進むには、狭過ぎて出入りするに困難な地形があります。この地形を隘（あい）（通路は隘路）といいます。隘の地形は、必ず先に占領、隘路口を封鎖して敵を待ち構えます。もしも敵が先にここを占領し、その狭隘口を防備、封鎖しているときは、攻撃してはなりません。敵が隘路口を封鎖していなければ、敵の動きに応じて攻撃します。

五　その山が険しく、また谷が深く堅固な地形があり、このような地形を険といいます。険の地形は、我が軍が先に占領して、必ず視射界良好な場所で敵を待ち構えます。もし敵が先に険の地を占領した時は、撤退して敵が誘ってきても、それに乗ってはなりません。

六　敵國深く突き進み、自国を出て甚だ遠い。このような所を遠地と呼び、戦闘を仕掛けてはなりません。敵味方が勢力均衡のときは、戦闘自体が不利益です。

Four

Both sides are in a narrows either between two mountains or in a valley where two mounted Samurai cannot ride abreast. This difficult kind of terrain and it is known as Ai, or cramped/narrow. When in Ai, cramped conditions, you must always occupy the area down the road, blocking off the entrance to the narrow passage known as Airo. From there you can wait for the enemy to approach. If the enemy has already occupied such a narrows and have fortified the entry point and sealed it off, then you absolutely should not attack. If the enemy has not sealed of the narrow passage then you should watch the enemy's movement for the best time to launch your attack.

Five

If the mountain is treacherous and the valleys around it deep and hard then the terrain is known as Ken, or dangerous and treacherous. In Treacherous terrain your army should always occupy the point with the best line of sight and wait there for the enemy. If the enemy occupies the Ken, or the best spot in treacherous terrain, you should withdraw your forces and ignore any attempts by the enemy to draw you out.

Six

You have moved deep into enemy territory and are very far from your own lands. Places like this are known as Enchi, or Distant Lands. You should never attempt any sort of trickery in such a place. When neither your side nor the enemy side has an advantage in battle, the whole affair is liable to be unprofitable.

遠形者勢均ケレハ難ス挑戦戦ニ云ニ而不利トヽ云

七 我國地力或ハ敵國ノ境ニ支未深後ニ能城
地十ト百方ニ引取ニヤスカ八ヘキ地形有是ヲ散
地或ハ軽地十ト、名付ヲ諸ニ平志ス曰人

六 戦スレハ不可有利ノ地形ト云也散地トハ謂
自戦其地人心易散謂之散地ニ云軽地トハ
人心軽返ノ之地七入敵國ノ境末深而吾城郭
天遠士卒心易於思返故謂之軽地ニ云

八 我此地ヲ取レハ呼方ニ得利敵此地ヲ取レハ敵

八　　　　　　　　　　　　　　　　　　　　　七

遠形者勢均ケレハ難以挑戰、戰テモ而不利ト云々

我国地力或ハ敵國ノ境ニ入事未深、後ニ能城

地ナト有テ引取ニヤスカルヘキ地形有、是ヲ散

地或ハ輕地ナトヽ名付テ諸卒志ヲ一ニメ

戰スンハ不可有利ノ地形ト云也、散地トハ謂

自戰其地、人心易散謂之散地云々、輕地トハ

人心輕返之地也、入敵國ノ境、未深而吾城郭

未遠士卒心易於思返故謂之輕地云々

我此地ヲ取レハ味方ニ得利、敵此地ヲ取レハ敵

七　我が領内か敵國との境で深く進軍しておらず、背後に我が城地があり、退却しやすい地形があります。これを散地或は、軽地と呼び、将士心を一つにして戦わなければ、不利となる地形といわれます。散地とは、総大将が自らその領内で戦うという意味で、心が乱れやすく、兵士の逃亡を誘う故に散地といいます。軽地とは、人心が軽く返る地、兵士が逃亡、帰郷したくなる土地であります。敵國にまだ深く侵入していなければ、我が城郭からまだ遠くありませんので、士卒の里心が湧きやすい故に軽地といいます。

八　我が軍がここを取れば、味方に有利になり、敵が取れば敵が有利になる地形があり、この地形を争地といいます。争地を先制している敵を攻撃してはなりません。

Seven

Your forces are still within your own territory or they have not entered deeply into enemy territory. Your own territory lies directly behind you and so it a situation easy to withdraw from. It is therefore known as Sanchi, Dispersal Territory or Keichi, Light (in the sense of easy) Territory. This type of territory is known for being difficult if the warriors on your side are not united in spirit. The reason it is known as Dispersal Territory is that the Overall Commander is fighting on his own lands, thus it is easy for his spirit to get into a jumble. Warriors are prone to being encouraged to flee and thus it is called Dispersal Territory. The reason for it being called Keichi is that it is easy for warriors' focus to be drawn back to their lands. Soldiers will flee or become overwhelmed with a desire to return home. If your army has yet to forge deep into enemy territory the feeling that your hometown is not so far away will be strong and as such feelings well up in your troops. That is why this terrain is known as Light Territory.

Eight

There is a kind of territory whereupon if the forces on your side take it over it will be a great advantage to your side. However, should the enemy take it over it will be a great advantage to their side. This kind of territory is known as Senchi, or Battlefield. You should never launch an attack against an enemy that has taken possession of such a place.

可得利地形百是ヲ爭地ト云ヲ爭地則無攻ト云

九 地形平ミニテカリレクル所十夕撤引自由ナル地

形百是ヲ交地ト云交地則勿絶或云吾將

謹其守ト云

十 四方ヨリノ通路多ノ敵味方其備ヲ出シヤ

スヘキ地形百是ヲ衢地ト云四通八達之所有援則成

無援則敗必其常合其交與國以為應援云

十一 敵國ヘ入フ甚深メ昧方國遠ク十死一生ノ地ヲ

名付テ重地ト云重地則掠云

九

利ヲ得ルベキノ地形アリ　コレヲ　ソウチ　トイウ　　争地即チセメナシ

可得利地形有、是ヲ争地ト云、争地則無攻ト云々

地形平ラニシテ隠レタル所ナクカケヒキジュウナルチ

地形平ニシテカクレタル所ナク掛引自由ナル地

ケイアリ　コレヲ　コウチ　トイウ　　交地則チ絶ツ勿レ　或ハ、ワガ将

形有、是ヲ交地ト云、交地則勿絶、或云吾将

十

謹ンデソレヲ守レト云々　々

謹 其守ト云々

シホウヨリノツウロ多クシテ敵味方ソノ備ヲイダシ

四方ヨリノ通路多メ敵味方其備ヲ出シ

ヤスキ地形アリ　コレヲクチ　トイウ　　四通八達ノ所、援ケ有ルトキ即チ成ル

ヤスキ地形有、是ヲ衢地ト云、四通八達之所有援則成

援ケ無キトキ敗ケル　　必ズ其ノ交ヲ合ス、当シ興スル国ヲ以ッテ応援為スス云々

無援則敗、必其當合其交與國以為應援云々

十一

敵国へ入ル事、甚ダ深クシテ味方国遠ク

敵國へ入事甚深メ味方國遠ク十死一生ノ地ヲ

名付テ重地ト云、　重地則チ掠ムト云々

名付テ重地ト云、重地則掠云々

九　地形が平らで障壁がなく進退がしやすい地形があり、この地形を交地といいます。交地では、各部隊間の連携を密にして絶やしてはなりません。或は、防御に遺憾なきを期すべきであります。

十　四方よりの通路が多く、敵味方共に動きやすい地形があります。この地形を衢地（みち）といい、四通八達（よんつうはったつ）故に同盟国からの援軍があれば勝利し、援軍がなければ敗軍となります。必ず近隣の諸国と同盟を組み、そして同盟関係をより密にして応援し合わなくてはなりません。

十一敵國へ甚だ深く侵攻して同盟国から遠く、十死に一生（じゅうし）の地を重地といいます。重地では、食料等の補給物資を掠奪して確保すべきです。

Nine

Due to its lack of obstructions there is a kind of terrain that is both easy to advance on and easy to withdraw from. This terrain is known as Kochi, or Interaction Terrain. When in Interaction Terrain communication and linking with each division should be complete and unbroken. On the other hand, if defending your preparations should be flawless.

Ten

Here there are connecting roads in all four directions. Since roads are prevalent it is easy to move on this terrain for both the forces aligned with you as well as the enemy. This terrain is known as Michichi, or Crossroads Territory. As there are a bewildering number of roads all over this terrain, if you receive reinforcements from neighboring aligned Domains you will achieve victory. Should such reinforcements fail to appear you will face defeat. You should always link up with adjoining Domains and form strong bonds. Without the aid that will come from such alignment you will not receive the reinforcements you need.

Eleven

Having advanced a great distance into enemy territory, you find yourself far from aligned domains. This kind of terrain wherein you have only the slimiest chance of emerging alive is known as Juchi, or Heavy Terrain. Should you find yourself in Juchi you should obtain food and other essentials by pillaging and plundering.

三ヶ大ハ七キ山路或ハ澤或ハ深田足入ナト多メ足場

大　惡キ地形ナ百是ッ名付テ圮地ト云圮地ハ無舎ニ云

圭　敵地ハ働入ル道切所ニシテ出入不自由ナル地形

百是ッ名付テ囲地ト云囲地則謀之云

古　故國深リ働入味方ノ國ヲハナシ敵ニ前後ノ

一　クシ粮道ヲタシ敵ニ得利ヲ味方ニハ失

一　其利進寺テ難成又引ヘキニテ便ナキ地形ッ

无地ト云死地ニハ示之不活又云疾戰則可

以存不疾戰則必亡云

十二 ケハシキ山路或ハ澤或ハ深田足入ナト多メ足場

ノ悪キ地形有、是ヲ名付テ圮地ト云、圮地ニハ 無 舎 云々

十三 敵地へ働入ル道切所ニシテ出入不自由ナル地形

有、是ヲ名付テ囲地ト云、囲地則謀之云々

敵國深ク働入、味方ノ國ヲハナレ、敵ニ前後ヲ

十四 カコマレ粮道ヲタ丶レ、敵ニハ得利地、味方ニハ失

其利、進事モ難成、又引ヘキニモ便ナキ地形ヲ

死地ト云、死地ニハ示之不活、又云疾戰則可

以テ存、不疾戰則必亡云々

185

十二　険しい山路や澤、深い水田、泥濘等の足場の悪い地形があります。この地形を圮_{やぶる}地といい、留まってはなりません。

十三　敵地へ侵攻する道が通行困難で出入りが不自由な地形があります。この地形を名付けて囲_{かこひ}地といい、囲地では謀略を謀る必要があります。

十四　敵國に進攻し、味方の國から離れ、敵軍に前後を囲まれ、粮道_{かてみち}を絶たれて敵軍に有利、味方に不利な土地で進む事も困難で、また退却にも困る地形を死地といいます。死地では、生還_{せいかん}が望めない事を部下に示し、迅速に全軍が必死奮闘して活路を開くべきです。迅速に全軍が奮戦敢闘しなければ必ず全滅すると心得るべきであります。

Twelve

Steep muddy mountain roads, deep rice paddies, mud combine to make a terrain with very poor footing. This type of ground is known as Yaburuchi, or Injured Terrain. You should never stop in such an area.

Thirteen

This type of terrain describes a path that, though it leads to the enemy's lands you are seeking to invade, it is difficult to pass though freely. It is known as Kakoichi, or Enclosure Terrain. You must consider your strategy carefully before venturing into such an area.

Fourteen

You have advanced into enemy territory and you are far away from any Domain that you have an alliance with. The enemy is both in front of you and behind you, completely encircling your forces. Your supply lines have been cut, giving the advantage to the enemy. This is a place where making for a friendly Domain is impossible and withdrawing would prove problematic. It is known as Shichi, or Death Terrain. You must inform your subordinates that there is no way to return home alive. The only course of action is for every member of the army to rapidly begin the fight and engage the enemy with all the ferocity they can in order to open a path out.

You should understand that without every member of the party immediately throwing themselves completely into the fray your forces will be annihilated.

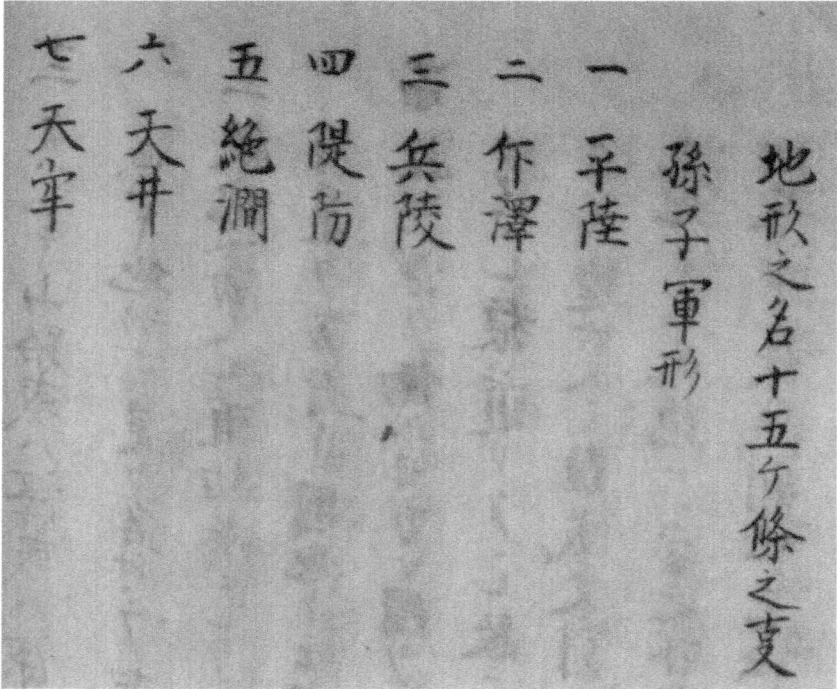

地形之名十五ヶ條之事

孫子軍形 ソンシグンケイ

地形 ノ 名 十 五 ヶ 条 ノ 事

一 平陸 ヘイリク

二 斥澤 セキタク

三 丘陵（キュウリョウ）
　 兵 陵

四 隄防 テイボウ

五 絶澗 ゼッカン

六 天井 テンセイ

七 天牢 テンロウ

地形之名十五ヶ條之事

孫子軍形

一　平陸…平坦な土地

二　斥澤…低湿地帯または、荒沢地

三　兵　陵…丘陵、小高い台地、丘

四　隄防…隄防や築堤、海岸や川岸などの水辺

五　絶澗…両側が切り立った深い谷などの激流、渡る事が困難な地形

六　天井…四方が高い山で湧き水が溜まる狭隘な盆地

七　天牢…谷の中に道が入り組み視界の悪い、いわば天然の牢獄

Fifteen Topics on the Names of Terrain

Terrain From Sun Tzu's Military Treatise.

One

Level Ground- Terrain that is more or less flat.

Two

Salty Swamp- An area that while there is water it is salty making for poor farming. Any area that is barren.

Three

Soldier's Hill- A mound, or slightly higher section of earth, a hill.

Four

Dike- A dike or earthen barrier by the ocean, river or other body of water.

Five

Precipice- A valley where both walls drop almost straight down with a violent rapids at the bottom. Very difficult to traverse terrain.

Six

Naturally Occurring Well- An area surrounded on all four sides by high mountains with water bubbling up into pools. Narrow terrain in a natural depression.

Seven

Naturally Occurring Prison- Within a valley the trails are twisting and intersecting, obscuring your line of sight. A natural prison cell.

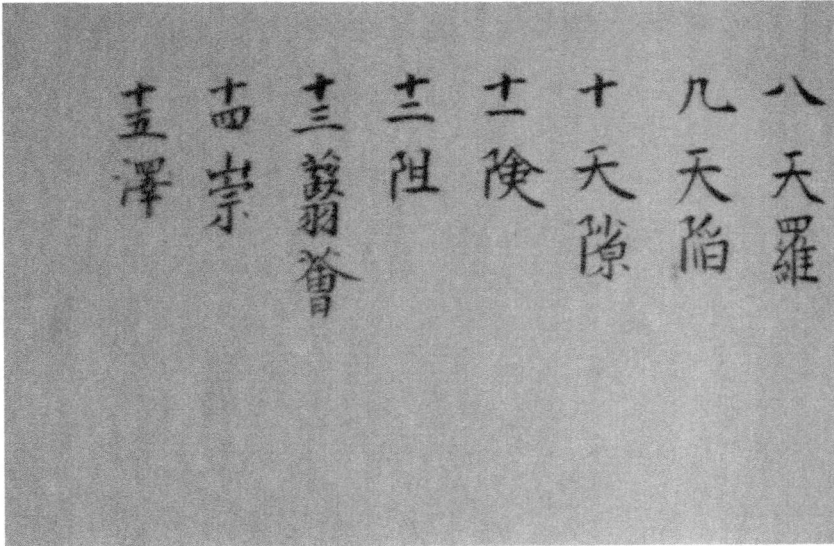

八 天羅
九 天陥
十 天隙
十一 険
十二 阻
十三 蘙薈
十四 崇
十五 澤

八　天羅　テンラ
九　天陥　テンカン
十　天隙　テンゲキ
十一　険　ケン
十二　阻　ソ
十三　蘙薈　エイワイ
十四　崇　ソウ
十五　澤　サワ

八　天羅…網目の如く草木が密生した森林・灌木地域

九　天陥…酷くぬかるんで足が沈み込み、足を取られる天然の罠のような沼沢地

十　天隙…穴や溝が多く足場の悪い地形、又は天然の裂け目のような狭い地形、一本道の隘路等

十一　険…起伏が激しく険しい地形

十二　阻…山間の水が多く広い湿原

十三　薈蔚…草木が覆い茂り、内部が見えない地形

十四　崇…かなりの高い所、高山

十五　澤…水が多く流れている不安定な湿地帯

Eight

Naturally Occurring Hunter's Net- A forest or shrubbery that the grasses and trees grow so densely together as to weave a net.

Nine

Naturally Occurring Pitfall- A muddy ground that sucks at the feet causing them to sink in deep. A natural trap for the legs.

Ten

Naturally Occurring Crevice- A type of terrain rife with holes, ditches and generally bad footing. Also refers to terrain that appears to be a natural crack, making one narrow trail.

Eleven

Harsh- A bumpy uneven and extremely dangerous terrain.

Twelve

Impede- Areas between mountains where water collects. Wide wet plains.

Thirteen

Obscure- A terrain that has undergrowth and trees so thick that they obscure the line of sight.

Fourteen

Worship- A high spot. A high mountain.

Fifteen

Swamp- A wetlands that has flowing water making footing very unstable.

あとがき

　武友のエリックさんより「兵法雄鑑巻十七〜巻廿」の印刷物を手渡されたとき、実に安請け合いしたものです。パッと見た目、楷書体で書いてあるし、中学高校の古文漢文のレベルで何とかなるだろうと高を括っておりました。

　しかし、やり始めてみれば、見たこともない漢字や変体仮名（楷書体であったものの『子』と書き、『ね』と読む）等、実に途方に暮れたものです。なんとか解読して現代語訳を作り、一旦手渡したものの、ややうやむやになり、ほったらかしにして時間を置いて見直せば、なんともはや恥ずかしい事に間違いだらけのなんのと再度苦戦…

変体仮名の解読に挑戦してオンライン閲覧ページで別の写本を解読したら、「宛」の読み方を間違えていたことも判明「あて」で良いかと思いきや「ずつ」でした…

意味合いも違ってしまいかねず、かなり焦りました。

　何だかんだ言っても勉強になる事、大で物事の考え方にも多少の影響があります。感謝感激雨霰であります。

　ありがとうございます。

飯田和寛

Afterward

When my Buyu, or martial arts friend, Eric (that's me) first handed me a printout of Heiho Yukan Vol. 17-20 I thought it was not going to be too much of a big deal. Just glancing at it the writing was not excessively ancient and seemed much like the old Japanese I studied in junior high school and high school.

However once I got into it I found all manner of Kanji and old style Kana alphabets that drove me up the wall. I gave it my all and was finally able to work out a modern Japanese translation. I turned the translation over and thought that would be the end of it. However as time passed I looked at it again and realized I had made all manner of embarrassing error. I began again in earnest...

By looking at different handwritten books online in my attempt to decipher the variations in Kana, I discovered that one Kanji that I felt positive was read as Ate was actually read Zutsu...As I did not want to make any errors in the meaning I began to panic a bit.

Despite everything it was a learning experience and ones way of thinking will no doubt influence the final product. All in all I am extremely grateful for this chance.

Thank you very much

Kazuhiro Iida

Books and Websites Used as Resource Material

参考文献ならびに参考サイト

- 「武家戦陣資料辞典」笹間良彦著　第一書房
- 「図説　日本戦陣作法辞典」笹間良彦著　柏書房
- 「面白いほどよくわかる孫子の兵法」杉之尾宣生監修 日本文芸社

- 戦国乱世を生きた人々…http://poliles.com/

- 兵法塾…http://www.heihou.com/index.htm

- 越後の虎〜武士の軌跡と史跡
  …http://26.pro.tok2.com/~yataro/index.htm

- 孫子の兵法 音声付…http://sonshi.roudokus.com/

- 中世歩兵研究所…http://www.geocities.co.jp/CollegeLife-Library/8740/index.html

- 知りたい歴史その答えはここにある
  …http://sakigakesamurai.blog46.fc2.com/

- みんなの知識ちょっと便利帳…http://www.benricho.org/

- 日本インターネット書道協会…http://www.nisk.jp/index.html

- 『木簡画像データベース・木簡字典』『電子くずし字字典データベース』連携検索…http://r-jiten.nabunken.go.jp/

- 孫子…http://www006.upp.so-net.ne.jp/china/book16.html
- 兵法雄鑑写本オンライン閲覧ページ
  …http://base1.nijl.ac.jp/iview/Frame.jsp?DB_ID=G0003917KTM&C_CODE=0281-091502&IMG_SIZE=&IMG_NO=1

- 『士鑑用法』にみられる北条氏長の武士観
  …https://www.jstage.jst.go.jp/article/budo1968/40/Supplement/40_1/_pdf

Printed in Dunstable, United Kingdom